Pocket
SEATTLE

TOP SIGHTS • LOCAL LIFE • MADE EASY

D0818703

Brendan Sainsbury

In This Book

QuickStart Guide

Your keys to understanding the city – we help you decide what to do and how to do it

Need to Know
Tips for a smooth trip

Neighborhoods
What's where

Explore Seattle

The best things to see and do, neighborhood by neighborhood

Top Sights
Make the most of your visit

Local Life
The insider's city

The Best of Seattle

The city's highlights in handy lists to help you plan

Best Walks
See the city on foot

Seattle's Best...
The best experiences

Survival Guide

Tips and tricks for a seamless, hassle-free city experience

Getting Around
Travel like a local

Essential Information
Including where to stay

Our selection of the city's best places to eat, drink and experience:

◉ **Sights**

✖ **Eating**

🍷 **Drinking**

✪ **Entertainment**

🔒 **Shopping**

These symbols give you the vital information for each listing:

☑	Telephone Numbers	👪	Family-Friendly
⊙	Opening Hours	🐾	Pet-Friendly
P	Parking	🚌	Bus
⊖	Nonsmoking	⛴	Ferry
@	Internet Access	Ⓜ	Metro
📶	Wi-Fi Access	🚝	Monorail
🌱	Vegetarian Selection	Ⓢ	Subway
📖	English-Language Menu	🚋	Tram
		🚆	Train

Find each listing quickly on maps for each neighborhood:

Bar Hemingway

16 📍 Map p233, B2

Legend has it that Hemi self, wielding a machine erate this timber-pan ered bar during showpiece is a en by Papa ar town. Dress s.com; Hôtel Rit ⊙ 6.30pm-2a

Lonely Planet's Seattle

Lonely Planet Pocket Guides are designed to get you straight to the heart of the city.

Inside you'll find all the must-see sights, plus tips to make your visit to each one really memorable. We've split the city into easy-to-navigate neighborhoods and provided clear maps so you'll find your way around with ease. Our expert authors have searched out the best of the city: walks, food, nightlife and shopping, to name a few. Because you want to explore, our 'Local Life' pages will take you to some of the most exciting areas to experience the real Seattle.

And of course you'll find all the practical tips you need for a smooth trip: itineraries for short visits, how to get around, and how much to tip the guy who serves you a drink at the end of a long day's exploration.

It's your guarantee of a really great experience.

Our Promise

You can trust our travel information because Lonely Planet authors visit the places we write about, each and every edition. We never accept freebies for positive coverage, so you can rely on us to tell it like it is.

QuickStart Guide 7

Explore Seattle 21

Worth a Trip:

The Best of Seattle   123

Seattle's Best Walks

Seattle's Best ...

Survival Guide   147

QuickStart Guide

Welcome to Seattle

Blink and it's changed: Seattle can be that ephemeral. Welcome to a city that pushes the envelope, embraces new trends and plots a path toward the future. But it's not all technological wizardry. Set on a jagged coastline amid emerald islands and snow-capped volcanoes, Seattle is handsome as well as precocious; a cultured slice of Pacific Northwestern splendor.

Seattle waterfront
CDRIN/SHUTTERSTOCK ©

Seattle
Top Sights

Pike Place Market (p26)

Way more than just a market, 110-year-old Pike Place is a living community, a cabaret show, a way of life and an intrinsic piece of Seattle's soul.

Space Needle (p56)

The city icon that is as synonymous with Seattle as the letters S-E-A-T-T-L-E was built for the 1962 World's Fair, and its novel revolving restaurant and bold futuristic design have proved durable.

Museum of Pop Culture (p60)

Paying homage to the left-handed, guitar-burning musical genius that was Jimi Hendrix, Paul Allen's architecturally bizarre MoPOP is an apt memorial in a region that has long been a powerful musical innovator. Pictured: *IF VI WAS IX* by sound sculptor Trimpin.

Museum of History & Industry (p74)

Seattle's history might not go back so far, but it's expertly curated in this cleverly redesigned naval armory building that sits attractively on the south shore of Lake Union.

Museum of Flight (p114)

The huge, super-modern Museum of Flight tells the remarkable tale of how humankind got from the Wright Brothers to the first moon landing in less than 66 years.

Discovery Park (p102)

Seattle justifies its 'Emerald City' moniker in the rugged confines of 534-acre Discovery Park, a one-time military installation reborn as a textbook example of urban sustainability.

Chihuly Garden & Glass (p58)

The US' capital of glass art offers up this imaginatively laid out set of galleries and gardens displaying the whimsical creations of local glass sculptor Dale Chihuly.

Seattle Art Museum (p24)

Seattle's art credentials are growing ever stronger thanks, in part, to this envelope-pushing downtown museum with dual specialties in modern and Native American art.

Pioneer Square Architecture (p42)

The homogeneous red-bricked neighborhood that served as Seattle's original downtown still reeks of history, intrigue and stories from the city's pioneering days.

Seattle Local Life

Insider tips to help you find the real city

After checking off Seattle's big-hitter sights, here's how you can experience what makes the city tick – the quiet local parks, hidden coffee corners, bohemian bars and envelope-pushing music venues that make up the Seattleite's Seattle.

Belltown, Old & New (p62)

▶ Bars
▶ Nightlife

For many people, Belltown is the pinnacle of Seattle's nightlife. Others dream nostalgically of the days when stage-diving was still an acceptable form of social interaction. Whichever view you hold, Belltown remains stuffed with strategically located places to eat, drink and listen to music.

Queen Anne Coffee Crawl (p76)

▶ Architecture
▶ Coffee

Coffee is practically a synonym for Seattle, and Queen Anne is the elegant quarter where many of the pioneering roasters and baristas confected their first lattes. Stroll past well-heeled mansions and drink in vast views as you taste the best brews the city has to offer.

A Musical Education in Capitol Hill (p86)

▶ Live music
▶ Clubbing

Those who walk through Capitol Hill quickly uncover its musical beat, whether it's pogoing to retro grunge in a punk pub or salsa-ing with a drag queen in a gay club. Tour the bars and dives of the Pike–Pine Corridor and listen out for the sound waves of Seattle's musical underground.

Parks & Pubs Around Lake Washington (p88)

▶ Parks
▶ Pubs

Beyond the Central District on Seattle's east side the city quickly melts into leafy suburbs interspersed with spacious parks overlooking Lake Washington. Once you're done with frolicking in the sun (or rain) with a frisbee, a host of cozy neighborhood pubs await.

Cheap Thrills on 'the Ave' (p90)

▶ Cheap eats
▶ Shopping

The U District is Seattle's proverbial student-ville, where the beautiful

Ferry to Bainbridge Island (p34)

University of Washington campus sits next to the shabbier 'Ave,' an eclectic strip of cheap boutiques, dive bars and ethnic restaurants for those on tight budgets.

Fremont Taste Tour (p94)

▶ Breweries
▶ Coffee

Fremont's restaurant scene is a regularly shuffled pack of cards with a few jokers thrown in. Locavore food is the latest niche. The neighborhood is also home to an excellent array of bars, taverns and brewpubs,

and is a good place to uncover Seattle's latest trends and zeitgeist.

Ballard's Bars & Beer Culture (p104)

▶ Bars
▶ Historic quarter

Ballard is Seattle's beer capital, which is saying something in a city that helped kick-start North America's 1980s microbrewing obsession. New bars and restaurants seem to pop up in the space of a lunch break, with fresh competition sitting alongside the dive bars of yore.

Other great places to experience the city like a local:

Bainbridge Island Ferry (p34)

First Thursday Art Walk (p46)

Owl & Thistle (p37)

Ballard Farmers Market (p110)

West Seattle Fish 'n' Chips (p119)

Salumi Artisan Cured Meats (p49)

Myrtle Edwards Park (p69)

Cheshiahud Loop (p80)

Fremont Almost Free Outdoor Cinema (p98)

Flip Flip Ding Ding (p120)

Seattle Day Planner

Day One

Early birds catch more than worms at **Pike Place Market** (p26). Arrive promptly at 9am for some real-life street theater at market roll call before wandering over to the Main Arcade to see the lippy fish throwers warming up. Spend the morning getting lost, browsing, tasting, buying and bantering with the producers, but don't miss the gum wall or Rachel the Market Pig.

When you're done wandering the market grab an on-the-go tub of mac 'n' cheese at **Beecher's Handmade Cheese** (p33) before tracking through Belltown to the Seattle Center where it'll take you exactly 41 seconds (by elevator) to zip up that other Seattle icon, the **Space Needle** (p56). After an hour of view-admiring and playing with the gadgets on top, descend to adjacent **MoPOP** (p60), where you can play on more gadgets (rock and roll this time) and immerse yourself in music memorabilia.

Dive back into Belltown for dinner at **Shiro's Sushi Restaurant** (p67) before continuing the rock theme at the **Crocodile** (p70), Seattle's grunge-throwback live-music venue.

Day Two

Return to Seattle Center for a stroll around this giant homage to the 1962 World's Fair taking in the finer details. Resist no longer the crystallized magnificence of **Chihuly Garden and Glass** (p58), one of the US' finest glass-art museums.

Divert into Belltown for lunch at lauded Europhile bistro **Tilikum Place Cafe** (p69). Walk along 6th Ave afterward and pop into the **Assembly Hall** (p63), where you can while away an hour drinking coffee or enjoying free games of pool and shuffleboard. See out the rest of the afternoon perusing modern art at the **Seattle Art Museum** (p24).

Go south for dinner, with a pint in Irish pub the **Owl & Thistle** (p37) and dinner in Pioneer Square Indian sensation, **Nirmal's** (p48). Should subterranean humor tempt you, head down the stairs to **Comedy Underground** (p52).

Short on time?
We've arranged Seattle's must-sees into these day-by-day itineraries to make sure you see the very best of the city in the time you have available.

Day Three

☀ Start the morning like a true Seattleite with a latte in **Zeitgeist Coffee** (p50), possibly the city's best indie coffee shop. Cross the road, admiring 1890s redbrick architecture, and visit the entertaining, educational and free **Klondike Gold Rush National Historical Park** (p46). If there's time, take a gilded-age elevator up the **Smith Tower** (p43) before lunch.

☀ Hit the International District for dim sum in **Jade Garden** (p50). Keeping with the Asian flavor: call in on the ID's most famous sight, the **Wing Luke Museum** (p46); and its most esoteric, the **Seattle Pinball Museum** (p46) for a quick game; before imbibing tea and Japanese American history in the **Panama Hotel Tea & Coffee House** (p50).

☾ In the evening work through our Musical Education in Capitol Hill local life tour (p86) and join Seattle's locavore culture with dinner at **Sitka & Spruce** (p129).

Day Four

☀ It's time for a journey through Seattle's outer neighborhoods. Start the morning in South Lake Union, where a lakeside park hosts the **Museum of History & Industry** (p74), a roller-coaster journey through Seattle's past.

☀ Have lunch in **Serious Biscuit** (p83), owned by celebrity chef Tom Douglas, before flagging a bus to Fremont. Soon after crossing the Fremont Bridge, you'll spy *Waiting for the Interurban* and plenty of other whimsical **public sculpture** (p127). Share coffee with the locals afterward at **Milstead & Co** (p99) before heading west by bus or bike to Ballard.

☾ Warm up in Seattle's best beer neighborhood with a microbrew in **Populuxe Brewing** (p110), before more rambunctious **King's Hardware** (p105), a remnant of Ballard's dive bars of yore. Louder still is the **Tractor Tavern** (p111), a legendary hive of indie rock and alt-country music.

Need to Know

For more information,
see Survival Guide (p147)

Currency
US dollar ($)

Language
English

Visas
Visa requirements vary widely for entry to the US and are liable to change. For up-to-date information, check www.travel.state.gov.

Money
ATMs are widely available. Credit cards are accepted at most hotels, restaurants and shops.

Mobile Phones
The US uses CDMA-800 and GSM-1900 bands. SIM cards are relatively easy to obtain.

Time
Pacific Standard Time
(GMT/UTC minus eight hours)

Plugs & Adaptors
Plugs have two vertical pins, electrical current is 120V. European visitors may need a transformer in addition to an adapter.

Tipping
Expected in most places
Bartenders and waitstaff 15% to 25%
Hotel porters $1 to $3 per bag
Taxi drivers 10% to 15%

① Before You Go

Your Daily Budget

Budget: Less than $125
► Dorm bed in a hostel: $25–35
► Pike Place Market take-out snacks: $3–6
► Certain days at museums: free

Midrange: $125–250
► Online deal at a no-frills hotel: $120–170
► Pub/bakery/sandwich bar meal: around $10
► Cheap tickets for sports games: from $12

Top end: More than $250
► Downtown hotel room: more than $200
► Meal at innovative restaurant: from $50
► Tickets to the theater or a concert: from $40

Useful Websites

The Stranger (www.thestranger.com) Seattle's best newspaper for entertainment listings – and it's free.

Seattle Weekly (www.seattleweekly.com) The city's other free newspaper can be picked up in coffee bars or metal street-side dispensers.

Lonely Planet (www.lonelyplanet.com/seattle) Information, hotel bookings and more.

Advance Planning

One month before Start looking at options for car rental, accommodations, tours and train tickets.

Two weeks before Whether you're hoping to see an opera performance or a Mariners game, it's wise to buy tickets in advance.

One to two days before Book popular restaurants. Search the *Stranger* and the *Seattle Times* for upcoming art and entertainment listings.

2 Arriving in Seattle

Seattle is served by Sea-Tac International Airport. Link light rail trains connect the airport with downtown Seattle. Amtrak trains use King Street station on the cusp of downtown.

✈ From Sea-Tac International Airport

Destination	Best Transport
Downtown	Light Rail Central Link
Pioneer Square	Light Rail Central Link
Seattle Center	Light Rail Central Link & Monorail
Belltown	Light Rail Central Link & walk

🚇 From King Street Station

Destination	Best Transport
Downtown	Light Rail Central Link
Georgetown	Bus 124
International District	Streetcar

3 Getting Around

There is a large and growing network of public transportation in Seattle. Fares are very reasonable. Light rail trains and streetcars have ticket machines at stations. For buses, pay on boarding.

M Metro

Regular all-day service on one light rail line between Sea-Tac airport and the University of Washington via downtown.

🚋 Tram

Two streetcar lines. South Lake Union line runs from Westlake Center to South Lake Union every 15 minutes. First Hill line runs from Pioneer Square to Capitol Hill. Fares are adult/child $2.25/1.50.

🚌 Bus

Run by King County Metro Transit (☏ 206-553-3000; www.metro.kingcounty.gov) on a wide number of routes. Buses are pay-as-you-enter and cost a peak-time flat fee of adult/child $2.75/1.50.

🚲 Bike

Seattle has a bike-sharing scheme called Pronto (☏ 844-677-6686; www.prontocycleshare.com) covering most of the central area. A 24-hour pass costs $8 payable at machines at any stations. You can also rent helmets.

🚤 Boat

A water taxi runs between Pier 50 on the waterfront to West Seattle, daily in summer, weekdays only in winter.

Seattle Neighborhoods

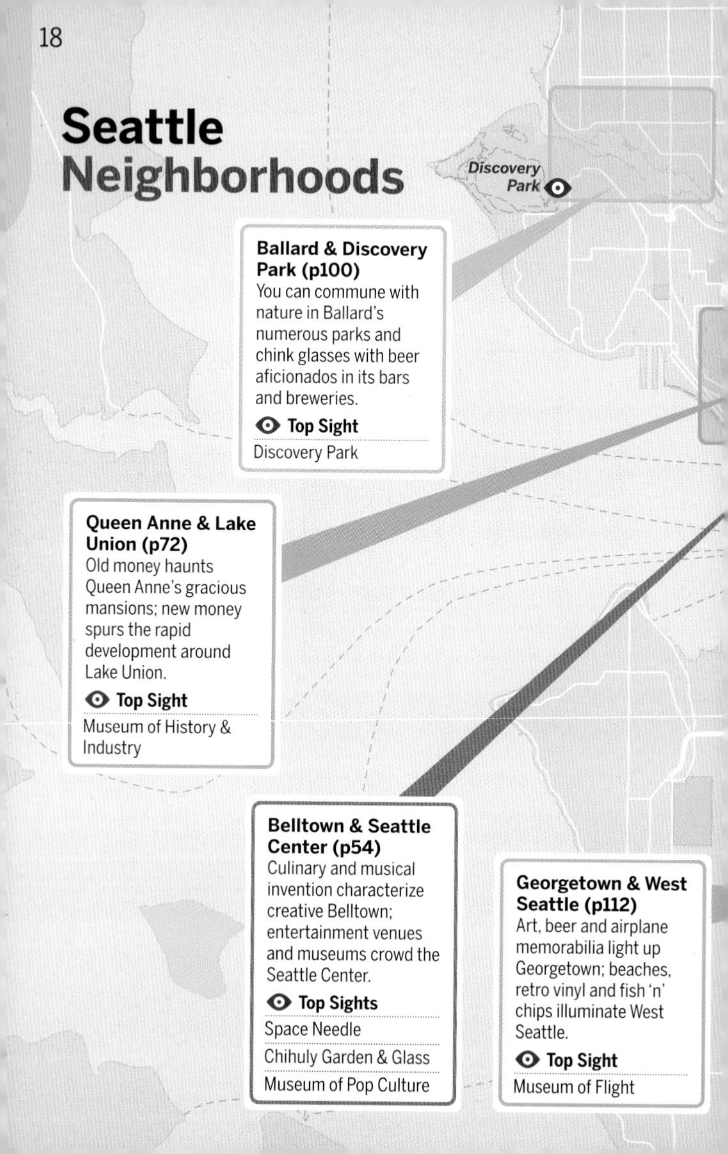

Discovery Park ◉

Ballard & Discovery Park (p100)

You can commune with nature in Ballard's numerous parks and chink glasses with beer aficionados in its bars and breweries.

◉ **Top Sight**

Discovery Park

Queen Anne & Lake Union (p72)

Old money haunts Queen Anne's gracious mansions; new money spurs the rapid development around Lake Union.

◉ **Top Sight**

Museum of History & Industry

Belltown & Seattle Center (p54)

Culinary and musical invention characterize creative Belltown; entertainment venues and museums crowd the Seattle Center.

◉ **Top Sights**

Space Needle

Chihuly Garden & Glass

Museum of Pop Culture

Georgetown & West Seattle (p112)

Art, beer and airplane memorabilia light up Georgetown; beaches, retro vinyl and fish 'n' chips illuminate West Seattle.

◉ **Top Sight**

Museum of Flight

Fremont & Green Lake (p92)
Fremont is off-beat and bizarre and proud of it; Green Lake is prettier but more sober.

Museum of History
👁 *& Industry*

Museum of Pop Culture
pace Needle
y Garden & Glass

Pike Place Market
👁👁 *Seattle Art Museum*
👁
Pioneer Square
Historical District

Downtown, Pike Place & Waterfront (p22)
Downtown's skyscrapers and department stores temper the brimming energy of one of the US' biggest and oldest farmers markets.

👁 **Top Sights**

Seattle Art Museum

Pike Place Market

Pioneer Square & International District (p40)
Seattle's oldest quarter offers a handsome ensemble of historic red-bricked buildings beside an atmospheric Asian quarter.

👁 **Top Sight**

Pioneer Square Historical District

Museum of 👁
Flight

Explore
SEATTLE

Worth a Trip

Seattle at sunset
CHECUBUS/SHUTTERSTOCK ©

Explore

Downtown, Pike Place & Waterfront

Downtown is a standard American amalgam of boxy skyscrapers and brand-name shopping opportunities that's given welcome oomph by Pike Place Market, the city's heart, soul and number-one sight for both locals and tourists. The waterfront, blemished since the 1950s by the soon-to-be-demolished Alaskan Way Viaduct, is undergoing a slow regeneration.

The Sights in a Day

☀ There's no better Seattle wake-up call than **Pike Place Market** (p26). Arrive early to beat the crowds and experience market roll call before disappearing off to explore the waterfront – more specifically, the strategically located **aquarium** (p32).

☀ Return to Pike Place for lunch, where you can graze from a variety of stalls and take-outs including **Beecher's Handmade Cheese** (p33). Grab a pastry dessert from **Piroshky Piroshky** (p33) and head for the **Seattle Art Museum** (p24) for modern artistic and Native American themes. You can integrate some shopping afterwards in the retail core, but don't get too weighed down before you've zipped up to the observatory deck of the **Columbia Center** (p32).

☾ Dump your shopping bag(s) in your hotel and return to Pike Place (yes, it's *that* good) for a warm-up cocktail in **Zig Zag Café** (p36). Several blocks away in downtown, you'll find the **Triple Door** (p37) offers some of the best dinner entertainment in the city, with food supplied by onsite restaurant, **Wild Ginger** (p34).

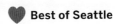

◉ Top Sights

Seattle Art Museum (p24)

Pike Place Market (p26)

♥ Best of Seattle

Eating
Piroshky Piroshky (p33)

Wild Ginger (p34)

Pink Door Ristorante (p34)

Crumpet Shop (p34)

Bars
Pike Pub & Brewery (p35)

Zig Zag Café (p36)

Owl & Thistle (p37)

Shopping
Pike Place Market (p26)

Metsker Maps (p38)

Market Magic (p39)

Tenzing Momo (p39)

Getting There

Ⓜ **Metro** Sound Transit's Link light rail from Sea-Tac Airport has two downtown stations: Westlake and University Street & 3rd Avenue.

🚋 **Tram** Streetcar service to South Lake Union from Westlake.

🚌 **Bus** You can get downtown easily from any part of Seattle by bus.

Top Sights
Seattle Art Museum

While not comparable with the big guns in New York and Chicago, Seattle Art Museum (SAM) is no slouch. Always re-curating its collection with new acquisitions and imported temporary exhibitions, it's known for its extensive Native American artifacts and work from the local Northwest School, in particular by Mark Tobey (1890–1976). It's spread across three sites: a **sculpture garden** (2901 Western Ave; admission free; ☼sunrise-sunset; 🚌13) in Belltown, an **Asian Art Museum** (1400 E Prospect St; adult/child $9/5, 1st Thu of month free; 🚌10) in Capitol Hill and this downtown campus.

◉ Map p30, C5

☎206-654-3210

www.seattleartmuseum.org

1300 1st Ave

adult/student $19.95/12.95

☼10am-5pm Wed & Fri-Sun, 10am-9pm Thu

🚃University St

Modern Art

SAM has an enviable collection of modern art. Level 3 is home to Andy Warhol's *Double Elvis*, a silk-screen image of a young Presley firing a pistol right at the viewer, and Jackson Pollack's drippy (and trippy) *Sea Change*.

Native American Art

The Hauberg Gallery on Level 3 is dedicated to the museum's impressive collections of items from Northwest coastal peoples, as well as Australian Aboriginal art and American and Native American textiles. Groups such as the Tlingit, Haida and Kwakwaka'wakw are all examined.

The Great Masters

Level 4 has a rather scattered collection of world art, from Greek pottery to the Italian renaissance. Standout pieces include *Pomponne Il de Bellièvre* by Van Dyck and *Saint Augustine in Ecstasy* by the Spanish baroque painter, Esteban Murillo. The 19th century is represented with works by Monet, Matisse and Vuillard.

Mark Tobey

One notable artist with multiple works on display in the Seattle Art Museum is Mark Tobey (1890–1976), an abstract impressionist with a penchant for Asian calligraphy who some view as an avant-garde precursor to Jackson Pollock. Works of Tobey to look out for include the dense, colorful *Festival* and the mask-etched *Esquimaux Idiom*, which has strong Native American undertones.

☑ Top Tips

▸ Entry to the museum is free on the first Thursday of every month.

▸ Your Seattle Art Museum ticket is also good for entry to the Seattle Asian Art Museum if used within one week.

▸ You can hear live jazz in the main entrance hall on the second Thursday of every month.

✖ Take a Break

SAM's excellent on-site restaurant, **Taste** (☎20 6-903-5291; www.tastesam. com; 1300 1st Ave; mains $15-25; ⊙11am-close Wed-Sat, 11am-5pm Tue & Sun), is far more comprehensive and elegant than your average gallery cafe. Sometimes it even creatively fine-tunes its menu to tie in with the art exhibits on show.

Top Sights
Pike Place Market

A cavalcade of noise, smells, personalities, banter and urban theater sprinkled liberally around a spatially challenged waterside strip, Pike Place Market is Seattle in a bottle. In operation since 1907 and still as soulful today as it was on day one, this wonderfully local experience highlights the city for what it really is: all-embracing, eclectic and proudly unique. Strolling through its clamorous, sometimes chaotic thoroughfares, you simply couldn't be in any other city.

Map p30, A4

www.pikeplacemarket.org

85 Pike St

9am-6pm Mon-Sat, 9am-5pm Sun

Westlake

Rachel the Pig

Stop and shake the bronze snout of Rachel the Market Pig in the main arcade, the de-facto mascot and presiding spirit of the market. This life-size piggy bank, carved by Whidbey Island artist Georgia Gerber and named after a real pig, collects about $10,000 each year. The funds are pumped back into market social services.

Main & North Arcades

The thin shedlike structures that run along the edge of the hill are the busiest of the market buildings. With banks of fresh produce carefully arranged in artful displays and fresh local fish piled high on ice, this is the real heart of the market. Here you'll see the famous fishmongers tossing salmon back and forth like basketballs.

Down Under

As if the levels of the market that are above ground aren't labyrinthine enough, below the Main Arcade are three lower levels called the Down Under. Here you'll find a fabulously eclectic mix of pocket-size shops, from Indian spice stalls to magicians supply shops and sellers of vintage magazines.

Corner & Sanitary Market

Across Pike Pl from the Main Arcade are the 1912 Corner & Sanitary Market Buildings, so named because they were the first of the market buildings in which live animals were prohibited. It's now a maze of ethnic groceries and great little eateries.

Post Alley

Between the Corner Market and the Triangle Building, narrow Post Alley (named for its hitching posts) is lined with shops and restaurants. In Lower Post Alley, beside the market sign, is the **LaSalle Hotel**, which was the first bordello north

---

☑ Top Tips

▶ If you dislike crowds, visit the market early (before 10am).

▶ Wander over to adjacent Victor Steinbrueck Park for beautiful clear-weather views of Mt Rainier.

▶ Join a Seattle **walking tour** (p145); plenty of them start in or around the market and all skillfully explain its history.

✕ Take a Break

You could spend half a day evaluating cheap eating options in Pike Place and get very hungry in the process. To save time, head to Beecher's Handmade Cheese (p33) for savory snacks (the mac 'n' cheese is a Seattle rite of passage) and Piroshky Piroshky (p33) for a sweet pastry afterwards. Both have perennial queues...and both are more than worth it.

of Yesler Way. The building, rehabbed in 1977, now houses commercial and residential space.

North End

The market's North End stretches along Pike Pl from Pine St to Victor Steinbrueck Park and is a popular meeting point for daily walking tours. The 1918 **Soames-Dunn building**, once occupied by a seed and a paper company, is now home to the world's oldest Starbucks. Beware of crowds and errant elbows knocking over your mermaid-logo coffee cup.

South Arcade

If you continue past DeLaurenti's Italian Deli, you'll come into the South Arcade, the market's newest wing, home to upscale shops and the lively Pike Pub & Brewery (p35). It's not technically part of the historic market but is with it in spirit and rambunctious energy.

Economy Market Building

Once a stable for merchants' horses, the Economy Market Building on the south side of the market entrance has a wonderful Italian grocery store and one of the oldest apothecaries on the West Coast. Look down at the Economy Market floor and you'll see some of its 46,000 tiles, sold to the public in the 1980s for $35 apiece.

The New MarketFront

In 2015 ground was broken on the 'Pike Up' project, a 30,000 sq ft extension of Pike Place. Made possible by the proposed demolition of the Alaska Way Viaduct, the new MarketFront complex contains shops, restaurants and stalls, and links the market to the waterfront via terraces, staircases and green space.

The Buskers

Anyone can busk in the market as long as they register with the market office, pay a $30 annual fee and perform in a designated spot. With a guaranteed annual audience of 10 million people, pitches are understandably popular. Well-known market performers include Johnny Hahn, who has been tickling the keys of an upright piano for nearly 30 years.

Gum Wall

Seattle's oddest and most unhygienic sight is the bizarre **gum wall** (Post Alley; [R] University St) situated at the southern end of Post Alley. The once venerable redbrick facade is now covered in used pieces of chewing gum, originally stuck there by bored theater-goers standing in line for a nearby ticket office in the 1990s. Add your own well-chewed morsels to the Jackson Pollock–like display.

Understand

History of Pike Place

Pike Place Market is the oldest continuously operating market in the nation. It was established in 1907 to give local farmers a place to sell their produce and bypass the middleman. Soon the greengrocers made room for fishmongers, bakers, ethnic groceries, butchers, cheese sellers and purveyors of the rest of the Northwest's agricultural bounty. The market wasn't exactly architecturally robust – it's always been a thrown-together warren of sheds and stalls, haphazardly designed for utility – and was by no means an intentional tourist attraction. That came later.

An enthusiastic agricultural community spawned the market's hey-day in the 1930s. Many of the first farmers were immigrants, a fact the market celebrates with annual themes acknowledging the contributions of various ethnic groups; past years have featured Japanese Americans, Italian Americans and Sephardic Jewish Americans.

Difficult Years

By the 1960s, sales at the market were suffering from suburbanization, the growth of supermarkets and the move away from local, small-scale market gardening. Vast tracts of agricultural land were disappearing, replaced by such ventures as Northgate Mall and Sea-Tac airport. The internment of Japanese American farmers during WWII had also taken its toll. The entire area became a bowery for the destitute and a center for prostitution.

Return to Prominence

In the wake of the 1962 World's Fair, plans were drawn up to bulldoze the market and build high-rise office and apartment buildings on this piece of prime downtown real estate. Fortunately, public outcry prompted a voter's initiative to save the market. Subsequently, the space was cleaned up and restructured, and it has become once again the undeniable pulse of down-town; some 10 million people mill through the market each year. Thanks to the unique management of the market, social-services programs and low-income housing mix with commerce, and the market has maintained its gritty edge. A market law prohibits chain stores or franchises from setting up shop and ensures all businesses are locally owned. The one exception is, of course, Starbucks, which gets away with its market loca-tion because it is the coffee giant's first outlet (it opened in 1971).

5th Ave

1 ❶
Columbia Center

Ⓡ Pioneer Square

3 Seattle Central Library ❸

5th Ave

4th Ave

Spring

3rd Ave

2nd Ave St

Columbia St

Marion St

1st Ave

PIONEER SQUARE

Cherry St

James St

Yesler Way

Ⓤ University Street

Washington Mutual Building

Post Ave

Western Ave

2nd Ave

Seneca St

Spring St

Madison St

WEST EDGE

17 ❾

1st Ave

Western Ave

Ⓧ Alaskan Way Viaduct

519

University St

Post Ave

Alaskan Way

Pier 53

Ⓢ Washington State Ferries

Pier 52

Pier 50

Ⓢ Water Taxis

Seattle Art Museum ❷

Western Ave

14 ❌

Alaskan Way Viaduct

Pier 55

Pier 54

Elliott Bay

Bainbridge Island

Bremerton

2 ❷ Aquarium
Pier 58

4 ❹ Pier 57
Seattle Great Wheel

Pier 56

E

D

C

B

A

5

6

7

8

Sights

Columbia Center VIEWPOINT

1 Map p30, E6

Everyone makes a rush for the iconic Space Needle, but it's not the tallest Seattle viewpoint. That honor goes to the sleek, tinted-windowed Columbia Center at 932ft high with 76 floors. An elevator in the lobby takes you up to the free-access 40th floor, where there's a Starbucks. From here you must take another elevator to the plush Sky View Observatory on the 73rd floor, from where you can look down on ferries, cars, islands, roofs and – ha, ha – the Space Needle! (☑206-386-5564; www.skyviewobservatory.com; 701 5th Ave; adult/child $14.25/9; ◷10am-8pm; ☒Pioneer Sq)

Seattle Aquarium AQUARIUM

2 Map p30, A5

Though not on a par with the city's nationally lauded Woodland Park Zoo (p97), the aquarium – situated on Pier 59 in an attractive wooden building –

is probably the most interesting site on the waterfront, and it's a handy distraction for families with itchy-footed kids. (☑206-386-4300; www.seattleaquarium.org; 1483 Alaskan Way, at Pier 59; adult/child 4-12yr $23/16; ◷9:30am-5pm; ☖; ☒University St)

Seattle Central Library LIBRARY

3 Map p30, E5

Rivaling the Space Needle and MoPOP with its architectural ingenuity, Seattle Central Library looks like a giant diamond that's dropped in from outer space. Conceived by Rem Koolhaas and LMN Architects in 2004, the $165.5 million sculpture of glass and steel was designed to serve as a community gathering space, a tech center, a reading room and, of course, a massive storage facility for its one-million-plus books. Come here to enjoy art, architecture, coffee and literary comfort. (☑206-386-4636; www.spl.org; 1000 4th Ave; ◷10am-8pm Mon-Thu, 10am-6pm Fri & Sat, noon-6pm Sun; ℗; ☒Pioneer Sq)

Seattle Great Wheel FERRIS WHEEL

4 Map p30, A5

With the Alaskan Way Viaduct soon to be confined to the 'ugly postwar architecture' chapter of the history books, Seattle has started work on beautifying its often neglected waterfront. Leading the way is this 175ft Ferris wheel that was installed in June 2012 with 42 gondolas, each capable of carrying eight people on a 12-minute

---

☑ Top Tip

Early Morning Market

Get to Pike Place Market (Map p30, A4) early and listen to the vendors chitchat as they set up their stalls. Be sure to witness the unique 'market roll call' in the North Arcade, when day-stall vendors are allocated their spaces.

Seattle Great Wheel

($13!) ride. (www.seattlegreatwheel.com; 1301 Alaskan Way; adult/child $13/8.50; ☺11am-10pm Mon-Thu, 11am-midnight Fri, 10am-midnight Sat, 10am-10pm Sun; 🚊University St)

Eating

Beecher's
Handmade Cheese   DELI $

 5 Map p30, A3

Artisan beer, artisan coffee...next up, Seattle brings you artisan cheese and it's made as you watch in this always-crowded Pike Place nook, where you can pick up all kinds of cheese-related paraphernalia. As for

that long, snaking, almost permanent queue – that's people lining up for the wonderful homemade mac 'n' cheese that comes in two different-sized tubs and is simply divine. (www.beechershandmadecheese.com; 1600 Pike Pl; snacks $3-5; ☺9am-6pm; 🚊Westlake)

Piroshky Piroshky   BAKERY $

 6 Map p30, A3

Piroshky Piroshky knocks out its delectable sweet and savory Russian pies and pastries in a space about the same size as a walk-in closet. Get the savory smoked-salmon pâté or the sauerkraut with cabbage and onion, and follow it with the choc-olate-cream hazelnut roll or a fresh

Local Life
Bainbridge Island Ferry

Tap the average Seattleite about their most cherished weekend excursion and they could surprise you with a dark horse – a cheap and simple ride on the commuter ferry to Bainbridge Island. There's nothing quite like being surrounded by water and seeing Seattle's famous skyline disappearing in the ferry's foamy wake. Catch the ferry from Pier 52 (Map p30, B7).

rhubarb piroshki. (www.piroshkybakery.com; 1908 Pike Pl; snacks $3-6; ⏱8am-6pm; 🚇Westlake)

Café Campagne   FRENCH $$

7   Map p30, A3

Short of teleporting over to Paris, this is about as Gallic as a Seattleite can get. Inside Café Campagne's effortlessly elegant interior you can live vicariously as a French poseur over steamed mussels, hanger steaks, generous portions of *frites* and crispy vegetables. Save room for the crème brûlée dessert. Should you be sufficiently satisfied, consider coming back for weekend brunch. (📞206-728-2233; www.cafecampagne.com; 1600 Post Alley; mains $16-29; ⏱11am-10pm Mon-Fri, 8am-11pm Sat, 8am-10pm Sun; 🚇Westlake)

Wild Ginger   ASIAN $$

8   Map p30, C4

All around the Pacific Rim – via China, Indonesia, Malaysia, Vietnam and Seattle, of course – is the wide-ranging theme at this highly popular downtown fusion restaurant. The signature fragrant duck goes down nicely with a glass of Riesling. The restaurant also provides food for the swanky Triple Door (p37) dinner club downstairs. (www.wildginger.net; 1401 3rd Ave; mains $17-33; ⏱11:30am-11pm Mon-Sat, 4-9pm Sun; 🚇University St)

Pink Door Ristorante   ITALIAN $$$

9   Map p30, A3

A restaurant like no other, the Pink Door is probably the only place in the US (the world?) where you can enjoy fabulous *linguine alle vongole* (pasta with clams and pancetta) and other Italian favorites while watching live jazz, burlesque cabaret, or – we kid you not – a trapeze artist swinging from the 20ft ceiling. (📞20 6-443-3241; www.thepinkdoor.net; 1919 Post Alley; mains $18-29; ⏱11:30am-10pm Mon-Thu, 11:30am-11pm Fri & Sat, 4-10pm Sun; 🚇Westlake)

Crumpet Shop   BAKERY $

10   Map p30, B4

The treasured British crumpet has been given a distinct American twist with lavish toppings such as pesto, wild salmon or lemon curd at this casual Pike Place Market eatery, family-owned and operated for almost 40 years. Organic ingredients make it very Pacific Northwest, though there's Marmite for homesick Brits. (📞20 6-682-1598; www.thecrumpetshop.com; 1503

1st Ave; crumpets $3-6; ⏱7am-3pm Mon, Wed & Thu, 7am-4pm Fri-Sun; ⓇWestlake)

Matt's in the Market NORTHWEST $$$

11 Map p30, B4

Matt's is perched above the bustle of Pike Place Market with views out over the famous clock, and oversees a menu where most of the ingredients come from down below. Expect plenty of fish, fresh veg and organic meats. For economy, come for the lunchtime sandwiches (the catfish is good). For fruity fish glazes and atmosphere, come for dinner. (☎206-467-7909; www.mattsinthemarket.com; 94 Pike St, Suite 32; lunch $15-18, mains $30-45; ⏱11:30am-2:30pm & 5:30-10pm Mon-Sat; ⓇWestlake)

Le Pichet FRENCH $$

12 Map p30, A3

Say *bonjour* to Le Pichet, just up from Pike Place Market, a cute and very French bistro with pâtés, cheeses, wine, *chocolat* and a refined Parisian feel. Dinner features delicacies such as wild boar shoulder or foie gras with duck eggs. (☎206-256-1499; www.lepichetseattle.com; 1933 1st Ave; mains $11-22; ⏱8am-midnight; ⓇWestlake)

DeLaurenti's FOOD $

13 Map p30, B4

A Pike Place Market veteran, this Italian grocery store/deli has been operated by the same family since 1946. Not needing to roll with the times, it offers a beautifully old-fashioned selection of wine, cheese, sausages, hams and pasta, along with a large range of capers, olive oils and anchovies. The sandwich counter is a great place to order panini, salads and pizza. (☎206-622-0141; www.delaurenti.com; 1435 1st Ave; snacks $5-12; ⏱9am-6pm Mon-Sat, 10am-5pm Sun; ⒓University St)

Ivar's Acres of Clams SEAFOOD $$

14 Map p30, B7

Ivar Haglund was a beloved local character famous for silly promotional slogans ('Keep clam!'), but he sure knew how to fry up fish 'n' chips. Ivar's is a Seattle institution that started in 1938, and its founder still stands sentinel at the door (albeit as a statue). (☎206-624-6852; www.ivars.com; 1001 Alaskan Way, Pier 54; mains $16-27; ⏱11am-9pm Sun-Thu, 11am-10pm Fri & Sat; 🚼; ⒓University St)

Drinking

Pike Pub & Brewery BREWERY

15 Ⓑ Map p30, B4

Leading the way in the US microbrewery revolution, this brewpub was an early starter, opening in 1989 underneath Pike Place Market. Today it continues to serve good pub food (mains $11 to $20) and hop-heavy, made-on-site beers in a busily decorated but fun multilevel space.

Free tours of the brewery are also available. (☎206-622-6044; www.pike-brewing.com; 1415 1st Ave; ⏱11am-midnight; ⓡUniversity St)

Zig Zag Café   COCKTAIL BAR

16 ⓟ Map p30, A4

If you're writing a research project on Seattle's culinary history, you'll need to reserve a chapter for Zig Zag Café. For serious cocktails, this place is legendary – the bar that re-popularized the gin-based Jazz Age cocktail, 'The Last Word,' in the early 2000s. The drink went viral and the Zig Zag's nattily-attired mixers were rightly hailed as the city's finest alchemists. (☎206-625-1146; www.zigzagseattle.com;

1501 Western Ave; cocktails from $8; ⏱5pm-2am; ⓡUniversity St)

Bookstore Bar   BAR

17 ⓟ Map p30, C6

Cementing downtown's reputation as a fount of good hotel bars is the Bookstore, encased in the front window of the Alexis Hotel, which mixes books stacked on handsome wooden shelves with whiskey – an excellent combination (ask Dylan Thomas). There are over 100 varieties of Scotch and bourbon available, plus a full gamut of weighty literary tomes from Melville to Twain. (☎206-624-4844; www.alexishotel.com; 1007 1st Ave; ⏱7am-midnight Mon-Fri, 8am-midnight Sat & Sun; ⓡPioneer Sq)

Understand
Starbucks – It Started Here – Almost

It's practically impossible to walk through the door of **Starbucks** (Map p30, A3; www.1912pike.com; 1912 Pike Pl; ⏱6am-9pm; ⓡWestlake) in Pike Place Market without appearing in someone's Facebook photo, so dense is the tourist traffic. But, while this hallowed business might be the world's oldest surviving Starbucks store, it is not – as many assume – the world's first Starbucks location, nor is it Seattle's oldest espresso bar. The original Starbucks opened in 1971 at 2000 Western Ave (at Western Ave's north end). It moved to its current location, a block away, in 1976. The honor of Seattle's oldest continuously running coffee bar goes to **Café Allegro** (p91) in the U District, which opened in 1975. Until the early 1980s Starbucks operated purely as a retail store that sold coffee beans and equipment (plus the odd taster cup). The company didn't open up its first espresso bar until 1984, after CEO Howard Schultz returned from an epiphanic trip to Italy. The Pike Place cafe is unique in that, in keeping with the traditional unbranded ethos of the market, it doesn't sell food or baked goods – just coffee.

Storyville Coffee
CAFE

18 Map p30, B4

There are so many coffee bars in Seattle that it's sometimes hard to see the wood from the trees, unless it's the kind of wood that adorns the curved bar of Storyville. Welcome to one of Seattle's newer luxury coffee chains, whose two downtown locations (here and at the corner of 1st and Madison) attract a mixture of tourists and locals who are looking for excellent coffee. (📞206-780-5777; www.storyville.com; 94 Pike St; ⏰6:59am-6pm; 🛜; 🚇Westlake)

Athenian Inn
BAR

19 Map p30, A4

There's nothing fancy about Pike Place Market's Athenian, but it's a landmark and a bastion of unpretentious, frontier-era Seattle. Consider, as you drink that hoppy beer, that this joint has been here since 1909, opening two years after the market itself. (📞206-624-7166; www.athenianinn.com; 1517 Pike Place Market; ⏰8am-8pm Mon-Thu, 8am-9pm Fri & Sat, 9am-4:30pm Sun; 🚇Westlake)

Tasting Room
WINE BAR

20 Map p30, A3

Pike Place Market is a good spot to sample the wares of some of Washington's best wine producers, and there are few better places than the Tasting Room, which offers four-glass tastings for $10. Friendly experts will talk you through the taste notes and tannins of prized vintages from Walla Walla,

Q **Local Life**

Owl & Thistle

Give the tourist bars a body-swerve and grab a pew at the harder-to-find Irish pub, the **Owl & Thistle** (Map p30, C7; 📞206-621-7777; www.owlnthistle.com; 808 Post Ave; ⏰11am-2am; 🚇Pioneer Sq), for Seattle's cheapest fish 'n' chips as well as inside info on the Sounders soccer chances.

the Yakima Valley and the Columbia River region. (📞206-770-9463; www.winesofwashington.com; 1924 Post Alley; ⏰noon-8pm Sun-Thu, noon-10pm Fri & Sat; 🚇Westlake)

Entertainment

A Contemporary Theatre
THEATER

21 ⭐ Map p30, E3

One of the three big theater companies in the city, the ACT fills its $30 million home at Kreielsheimer Pl with performances by Seattle's best thespians and occasional big-name actors. Terraced seating surrounds a central stage, and the interior has gorgeous architectural embellishments. (ACT; 📞206-292-7676; www.acttheatre.org; 700 Union St; 🚇University St)

Triple Door
LIVE PERFORMANCE

This club (see **8** ✕ Map p30, C4) downstairs from the Wild Ginger (p34) restaurant is a Seattle mainstay with a liberal booking policy that includes country and rock as well as jazz, gospel, R&B, world music and burlesque performances. There's a full menu and a smaller lounge upstairs called the **Musicquarium** with an aquarium and free live music. (📞20 6-838-4333; www.thetripledoor.net; 216 Union St; 🚇University St)

Seattle Symphony CLASSICAL MUSIC

22 ⭐ Map p30, C4

A major regional ensemble, the Seattle Symphony orchestra plays at the **Benaroya Concert Hall** (📞20 6-215-9494; 200 University St), which you'll find downtown at 2nd Ave and

Pike Pub & Brewery (p35)

University St. (www.seattlesymphony.org; 🚇University St)

5th Avenue Theater THEATER

23 ⭐ Map p30, D4

Built in 1926 with an opulent Asian motif, the 5th Avenue opened as a vaudeville house; it was later turned into a movie theater and then closed in 1979. An influx of funding and a heritage award saved it in 1980, and now it's Seattle's premier theater for Broadway musical revivals. It's worth going just for a look at the architecture. (📞206-625-1900; www.5thavenue.org; 1308 5th Ave; ⏱box office 9:30am-5:30pm Mon-Fri; 🚇University St)

Shopping

Old Seattle Paperworks POSTERS, MAGAZINES

24 🔒 Map p30, A4

If you like decorating your home with old magazine covers from *Life, Time* and *Rolling Stone,* or have a penchant for art-deco tourist posters from the 1930s, or are looking for that rare Hendrix concert flyer from 1969, this is your nirvana. It's in Pike Place Market's Down Under section. (1501 Pike Place Market, downstairs; ⏱10:30am-5pm; 🚇Westlake)

Metsker Maps MAPS

25 🔒 Map p30, B4

In its high-profile location on 1st Ave, this 65-year-old map shop sells all kinds of useful things for the traveler, from maps to guidebooks to various accessories. It also has a good selection of armchair-travel lit and pretty spinning globes for the dreamers. (☎206-623-8747; www.metskers.com; 1511 1st Ave; ⊙9am-8pm Mon-Fri, 10am-8pm Sat, 10am-6pm Sun; ᴿWestlake)

Market Magic
MAGIC

26 Map p30, A4

Selling fake dog turds, stink bombs, water-squirting rings and magic tricks, this Pike Place Market magic shop is heaven for aspiring magicians, pranksters, school kids, and grown-ups who wish they were still school kids. (☎206-624-4271; www.marketmagicshop.com; 1501 Pike Pl, No 427; ⊙10am-5pm; ᴿWestlake)

Tenzing Momo
GIFTS & SOUVENIRS

27 Map p30, B4

Doing a good impersonation of one of the magic shops in Diagon Alley from the *Harry Potter* books, Tenzing Momo is an old-school natural apothecary with shelves of mysterious glass bottles filled with herbs and tinctures to treat any ailment. (☎206-623-9837; www.tenzingmomo.com; Economy Market Bldg, Pike Place Market; ⊙10am-6pm; ᴿUniversity St)

Pure Food Fish
FOOD

28 Map p30, B4

Perhaps the gift that says 'I heart Seattle' the most is a whole salmon or other fresh seafood from the fish markets. All the markets will prepare fish for transportation on the plane ride home but Pure Food Fish has been around for four generations and has the best reputation for quality and value. (☎206-622-5765; www.freshseafood.com; 1511 Pike Pl; ⊙9am-5pm; ᴿWestlake)

Nordstrom
DEPARTMENT STORE

29 Map p30, C2

Born and raised in Seattle by a Klondike gold-rush profiteer, this upmarket department store occupies a giant space in the former Frederick and Nelson Building. In the Westlake Center, the more economical **Nordstrom Rack** (☎206-448-8522; 400 Pine St; ⊙9:30am-9pm Mon-Sat, 10am-8pm Sun; ᴿWestlake) offers close outs and returns from the parent store. (☎206-628-2111; www.nordstrom.com; Pine St, btwn 5th & 6th Aves; ⊙9:30am-9pm Mon-Sat, 10am-7pm Sun; ᴿWestlake)

Explore

Pioneer Square & International District

Seattle's birthplace retains the grit of its 'Skid Row' roots with historic redbrick architecture and a rambunctious street life tempered by art galleries and locavore restaurants. It's known primarily for its monthly art walk and giant sports stadiums directly to the south. The International District is a Chinese/Vietnamese neighborhood that broadcasts its scruffy cosmopolitanism with dim sum and *pho* restaurants.

The Sights in a Day

☀ Grey skies or blue, your plans for the day will quickly become clearer after a coffee at **Zeitgeist** (p50). Pioneer Square is a place to stroll and sit, pondering the attractive architecture, epoch-defining history and theatrical modern street life. Drink in the decorative embellishments of **Pioneer Square Park** (p48), ride the gilded elevator up **Smith Tower** (p43) and enjoy fact-packed, free **Klondike Gold Rush National Historical Park** (p46).

☼ If the weather is smiling, linger for lunch in recently beautified **Occidental Park** (p46), where food carts pull up and outdoor games (ping pong anyone?) pitch locals against tourists. Next, take a short walk over to the International District for an obligatory pick-me-up in the **Panama Hotel** (p50) and snippets of Seattle's immigration stories at the **Wing Luke Museum of the Asian Pacific American Experience** (p46).

☽ Linger in the ID for an Asian-themed dinner. The *pho* and chunky spring rolls at **Tamarind Tree** (p49) are legendary. Head back over to Pioneer Square for an evening of edgy amusement in the **Comedy Underground** (p52).

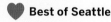

👁 Top Sights

Pioneer Square Historical District (p42)

💜 Best of Seattle

Coffee Spots
Zeitgeist Coffee (p50)

Caffè Umbria (p51)

Spectator Sports
CenturyLink Field (p51)

Safeco Field (p51)

For Free
Pioneer Square Historical District (p42)

Klondike Gold Rush National Historical Park (p46)

Occidental Park (p46)

Getting There

Ⓜ **Metro** Link light rail from Seattle-Tacoma Airport stops at Pioneer Sq station or International District/Chinatown station. It carries on to Westlake Station in downtown and, ultimately, the U District.

🚋 **Tram** Runs from S Jackson St in Pioneer Sq through the ID, CD and First Hill to Capitol Hill.

Top Sights
Pioneer Square Historical District

Many important architectural heirlooms are concentrated in Pioneer Sq, the district that sprang up in the wake of the 1889 Great Fire. Instantly recognizable by its handsome redbrick buildings, the neighborhood's predominant architectural style is Richardsonian Romanesque, strongly influenced by America's Chicago School. Nearly destroyed by overzealous city planners in the 1960s, the district was saved by a group of foresighted historical preservationists who were instrumental in getting the neighborhood listed as a historic district in 1970.

 Map p44, C1

btwn Alaskan Way S, S King St, 5th Ave S, 2nd Ave ext & Columbia St

🚇 Pioneer Sq

Pioneer Building

Pioneer Building

Built in 1891, the magnificent **Pioneer Building** (606 1st Ave S) facing Pioneer Square Park is one of the finest Victorian buildings in Seattle and showcases many of the classic components of Richardsonian Romanesque; look for the Roman arches, a recessed main doorway, curvaceous bay windows and decorative flourishes: most notably the two frontal columns with embellished bricks.

Grand Central Arcade

The lovely **Grand Central Arcade** (206-623-7417; 214 1st Ave S; Occidental Mall) was originally Squire's Opera House, erected in 1879. When the Opera House was destroyed in the Great Fire it was rebuilt as the Squire-Latimer Building in 1890 and later became the Grand Central Hotel. The hotel died during the Depression. The restored building now contains two floors of shops.

Smith Tower

A mere dwarf amid Seattle's impressive modern stash of skyscrapers, the 42-story neoclassical **Smith Tower** (206-622-4004; www.smithtower. com; 506 2nd Ave) was, for half a century after its construction in 1914, the tallest building west of Chicago. The beaux-arts-inspired lobby is onyx- and marble-paneled. A brass-and-copper elevator takes you up to the observation deck on the 35th floor.

Richardsonian Romanesque

Pioneer Sq's hallmark architecture is a revivalist style from the 1880s that harks back to the medieval European genre of Romanesque, in vogue from the 10th to the 12th centuries. Features of Richardsonian Romanesque include classical Roman arches, heavy rough-cut masonry, recessed doorways, and the use of decorative columns and bricks.

☑ **Top Tips**

▶ Choose a fine day and you can soak up the atmosphere of Pioneer Sq while sitting in the once gritty, but now pretty, Occidental Park.

▶ To get the full lowdown on the buildings, you'll need to get underneath them in one of several subterranean **tours** (p145).

▶ There's a handy information kiosk giving out neighborhood maps in Occidental Park.

✗ **Take a Break**

Pioneer Sq is crammed with cheap places to rest your weary legs. For coffee and some rather good almond croissants, tune into the neighborhood zeitgeist at **Zeitgeist Coffee** (p50). For excellent take-out salads, raid the deli counter at **London Plane** (p48).

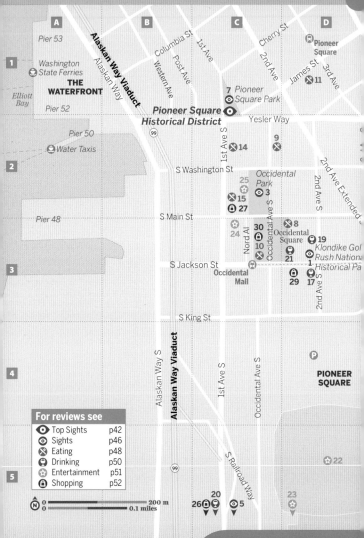

Pier 53

A

Washington
State Ferries
**THE
WATERFRONT**

B

Columbia St

Post Ave

1st Ave

Western Ave

Alaskan Way Viaduct

Alaskan Way

C

Cherry St

2nd Ave

D

Pioneer
Square

James St

3rd Ave

1

Elliott
Bay

Pier 52

7 Pioneer
Square Park

**Pioneer Square
Historical District**

Yesler Way

11

Pier 50

Water Taxis

99

1st Ave S

14

9

S Washington St

*Occidental
Park*

2nd Ave Extended

2

25

15
27

3

2nd Ave S

Pier 48

S Main St

24

Nord Al

30
10

8

Occidental
Square

19

Occidental Ave S

21

Klondike Gol
Rush Nationa
Historical Pa

1

3

S Jackson St

**Occidental
Mall**

29

17

2nd Ave S

S King St

Alaskan Way S

1st Ave S

Occidental Ave S

P

**PIONEER
SQUARE**

4

For reviews see

⊙	Top Sights	p42
⊙	Sights	p46
✕	Eating	p48
🍷	Drinking	p50
✿	Entertainment	p51
🔒	Shopping	p52

N

0   200 m
0   0.1 miles

99

S Railroad Way

20
26

5

22

23

5

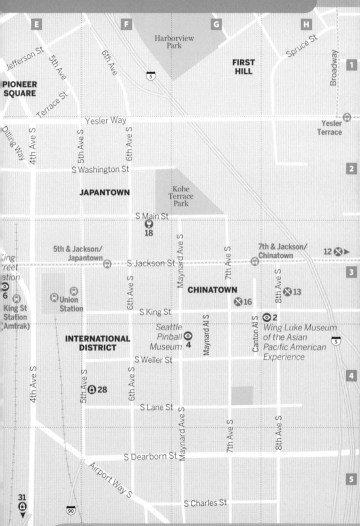

E   F   G   H

Jefferson St

5th Ave

6th Ave

Spruce St

Broadway

Harborview Park

FIRST HILL

PIONEER SQUARE

Terrace St

Dilling Way

Yesler Way

Yesler Terrace

4th Ave S

5th Ave S

6th Ave S

S Washington St

JAPANTOWN

Kobe Terrace Park

S Main St
18

5th & Jackson/ Japantown

Maynard Ave S

7th Ave S

7th & Jackson/ Chinatown

12

King reet ation

6

S Jackson St

8th Ave S

13

King St Station (Amtrak)

Union Station

6th Ave S

5th Ave S

S King St

Maynard Al S

CHINATOWN

16

Canton Al S

2

INTERNATIONAL DISTRICT

Seattle Pinball Museum 4

Maynard Ave S

Wing Luke Museum of the Asian Pacific American Experience

4th Ave S

5th Ave S

6th Ave S

S Weller St

28

S Lane St

7th Ave S

8th Ave S

S Dearborn St

Maynard Ave S

Airport Way S

31

90

S Charles St

Sights

Klondike Gold Rush
National Historical Park   MUSEUM

1 Map p44, D3

This wonderful museum eloquently run by the US National Park Service has exhibits, photos and news clippings from the 1897 Klondike gold rush, when a Seattle-on-steroids acted as a fueling depot for prospectors bound for the Yukon in Canada. It would cost $20 entry anywhere else; in Seattle it's free! (☎206-553-3000; www.nps.gov/klse; 319 2nd Ave S; admission free; ⏱10am-5pm; 🚇Occidental Mall)

Wing Luke Museum
of the Asian Pacific
American Experience   MUSEUM

2 Map p44, H3

The beautifully unique Wing Luke examines Asian-Pacific American

culture, focusing on prickly issues such as Chinese settlement in the 1880s and Japanese internment camps during WWII. There are also art exhibits and a preserved immigrant apartment. Guided tours are available; the first Thursday of the month is free (with extended hours until 8pm). (☎206-623-5124; www.wingluke.org; 719 S King St; adult/child $15/10; ⏱10am-5pm Tue-Sun; 🚇7th & Jackson/Chinatown)

Occidental Park   PARK

3 Map p44, C2

Once a rather grim place, Occidental Park has undergone a recent renaissance thanks largely to a partnership between the City of Seattle and a couple of non-profit groups. Following an urban renewal campaign in 2015, the park has been kitted out with attractive seating, outdoor games (including chess and table football), licensed buskers and a regular posse of food carts. (btwn S Washington & S Main Sts; 🚇Occidental Mall)

Seattle
Pinball Museum   MUSEUM, GAMES

4 Map p44, G4

Got kids? Got kidlike tendencies? Love the buzzers and bells of old-fashioned game machines? Lay aside your tablet apps and become a pinball wizard for the day in this fantastic games room in the ID with machines from 1960 retro to 2015 futuristic. Admission buys you unlimited games for the day. Sure plays a mean pinball! (☎206-623-0759; www.seattlepinballmuseum.com; 508 Maynard

---

Local Life
First Thursday Art Walk

Pioneer Square's **art walk** (www.firstthursdayseattle.com) claims to be the oldest in the nation and a creative pathfinder for all that followed. Aside from gluing together the neighborhood's network of 50-plus galleries, the walk is a good excuse to admire creative public sculpture, browse an array of stalls set up in Occidental Park, and get to know the neighborhood and its people.

Wing Luke Museum of the Asian Pacific American Experience

Ave S; adult/child 7-12yr $13/10; ⊘noon-5pm Mon, Wed & Sun, noon-10pm Thu-Sat; ✦; ⛟7th & Jackson/Chinatown)

Living Computer Museum
MUSEUM

5 ◉ Map p44, C5

Owned by unapologetic computer geek and Microsoft co-founder, Paul Allen, this place will evoke heavy nostalgia in anyone who can remember the world pre-internet. Hosted in a nondescript commercial building in industrial SoDo and little known even among locals, it's well worth checking out for its host of antediluvian computers with their blinking green cursors and black, app-free screens. Some of them are large enough to fill an average-sized student bedroom. (www.livingcomputer museum.org; 2245 1st Ave S; adult/child $6/2; ⊘10am-5pm Wed-Sun; ⛟SoDo)

King Street Station
LANDMARK

6 ◉ Map p44, E3

One of the pillars upon which Seattle built its early fortunes, the old Great Northern Railroad depot was given some much needed Botox in the early 2010s after decades of neglect. Serving as the western terminus of the famous Empire Builder train that runs between Seattle and Chicago, the station building was designed to imitate St Mark's bell tower in Venice. (303 S Jackson St; ⛟International District/Chinatown)

Pioneer Square Park SQUARE

 7 Map p44, C1

The original Pioneer Square is a cobbled triangular plaza where Henry Yesler's sawmill cut the giant trees that marked Seattle's first industry. Known officially as Pioneer Square Park, the plaza features a bust of **Chief Seattle** (Sealth, in the original language), an ornate **pergola** (cnr Yesler Way & James St) and a **totem pole**. (cnr Cherry St & 1st Ave S; Pioneer Sq)

Eating

London Plane CAFE, DELI $$

 8 Map p44, D3

Matt Dillon (the Seattle chef, not the Hollywood actor) moved less than a block from his established restaurant, **Bar Sajor**, to open London Plane, a hybrid cafe, flower shop, deli and breakfast spot that maintains the French country kitchen feel that has become Dillon's trademark. (20 6-624-1374; www.thelondonplaneseattle.com; 300 Occidental Ave S; small plates $7-20; 8am-5pm Mon-Tue, 8am-9pm Wed-Fri, 9am-9pm Sat, 9am-5pm Sun; Occidental Mall)

Nirmal's INDIAN $$$

9 Map p44, C2

At last...Seattle has filled a massive hole in its culinary resume – good Indian food. Nirmal's is a brave new restaurant that takes a stab at pretty much any flavor under the South Asian umbrella, be it Goan fish curry, Bengali prawns or Kashmiri rack of lamb. (206-388-2196; www.nirmal seattle.com; 106 Occidental Ave S; mains $15-30; 11am-2pm Mon-Wed, 11am-2pm & 5:30-10pm Thu & Fri, 5:30-10pm Sat; Pioneer Sq)

Bar Sajor MEDITERRANEAN $$

 10 Map p44, C3

Resembling a bright, open-plan French country kitchen and claiming to serve Portuguese-inspired food created from the raw ingredients of Seattle's hinterland, Bar Sajor is a project from Matt Dillon, who built his reputation at Capitol Hill's hugely popular (and sustainable) **Sitka & Spruce** (p129). (206-682-1117; www. barsajor.com; 323 Occidental Ave; plates $10-25; 4-9:30pm Tue-Fri, 10am-2pm & 4-9:30pm Sat, 10am-2pm & 5:30-9pm Sun; Occidental Mall)

Il Corvo Pasta ITALIAN $

11 Map p44, D1

A unique hole-in-the-wall, pasta-only place with limited seating and a high turnover of office workers on their lunch breaks. Join the perennial queue, order one of three daily pastas with sauces and grab a seat (if there's one available). You have to bus your own table, Seattle-style, at the end. Wine and bread provide welcome accompaniments. (20 6-538-0999; www.ilcorvopasta.com; 217 James St; pasta $10; 11am-3pm Mon-Fri; Pioneer Sq)

Tamarind Tree

VIETNAMESE $$

12 Map p44, H3

Serving upscale food at lowbrow prices in a massively popular dining room, this legendary place has a nuanced menu that includes everything from satays and salad rolls to big bowls of *pho* and rice cakes (squid-, prawn- and pork-filled fried crepes). It also donates some of its profits to the Vietnam Scholarship Foundation. It's hidden at the back of an ugly car park. (☑206-860-1414; www.tamarindtreerestaurant.com; 1036 S Jackson St; mains $12-17; ☑10am-10pm Sun-Thu, 10am-midnight Fri & Sat; ☒Little Saigon)

Green Leaf

VIETNAMESE $

13 Map p44, H3

Popular Green Leaf, located in Chinatown, shoots out rapid-fire dishes from its tiny kitchen that abuts a dining room not much wider than a railway carriage. Choose the traditional *pho* (beef noodle soup) or go for the excellent rice- or vermicelli-noodle dishes – especially the *bún dắc biệt* (with pork, chicken and shrimp). There's also a branch in Belltown at 2800 1st Ave. (☑206-340-1388; www.greenleaftaste.com; 418 8th Ave S; pho $9, specials $10-12; ☑11am-10pm; ☒7th & Jackson/Chinatown)

Damn the Weather

MODERN AMERICAN $$

14 Map p44, C2

Repeating a mantra that flows freely from the lips of many Seattleites,

this new-ish venture is perhaps best described as a cocktail bar that also serves damn good food. The interior is typical Pioneer Square – all wooden floors, bare-brick walls and low-lit chandeliers – while the clientele is a blend of hipsters meets yuppies on their way home from the office. (☑206-946-1283; www.damntheweather.com; 116 1st Ave S; small plates $8-12; ☑4pm-2am Mon-Sat, 4-11pm Sun; ☒Occidental Mall)

Grand Central Baking Co

SOUP, SANDWICHES $

15 Map p44, C2

Grand Central (located in the eponymous building) is considered one of the best bakeries in Seattle. Its artisan breads can be bought whole or sliced up for sandwiches in its cafe and enjoyed in the redbrick confines of the Grand Central mall, or at a Euro-chic table in Occidental Park (p46) outside. Beware the lunchtime queues. (☑206-622-3644; www.grandcentralbakery.com;

CenturyLink Field

Grand Central Arcade, 214 1st Ave S; sandwiches $4-10; ⏲7am-5pm Mon-Fri, 8am-4pm Sat; Occidental Mall)

Jade Garden
CHINESE $

16 Map p44, G3

Usually mentioned near the top of the list of best places for dim sum in the ID, Jade Garden offers a good range of delicacies with everything from standard, newbie-friendly shrimp dumplings and steamed pork buns to more exotic plates such as black cylinders of sesame-paste gel and, of course, chicken's feet. The more things you try, the more fun you'll have. (📞206-622-8181; 424 7th Ave S; dim-sum items $2-3, mains $8-12; ⏲10am-2:30am; 🚌7th & Jackson/Chinatown)

Drinking

Zeitgeist Coffee
CAFE

17 🚇 Map p44, D3

Possibly Seattle's best indie coffee bar, Zeitgeist brews up smooth *doppio macchiatos* to go along with its sweet almond croissants and other luscious baked goods. The atmosphere is trendy industrial, with brick walls and large windows for people-watching. Soups, salads and sandwiches are also on offer. (📞206-583-0497; www.zeitgeist coffee.com; 171 S Jackson St; ⏲6am-7pm Mon-Fri, 7am-7pm Sat, 8am-6pm Sun; 📶; 🚌Occidental Mall)

Panama Hotel Tea & Coffee House
CAFE

18 🚇 Map p44, F3

The Panama, a historic 1910 building containing the only remaining Japanese bathhouse in the US, doubles as a memorial to the neighborhood's Japanese residents forced into internment camps during WWII. The beautifully relaxed cafe has a wide selection of teas, serves Lavazza Italian coffee and holds a National Treasure designation. (📞206-515-4000; www.panamahotel.net; 607 S Main St; ⏲8am-9pm; 🚌5th & Jackson/Japantown)

88 Keys Dueling Piano Bar
BAR

19 🚇 Map p44, D3

Reviving the almost lost art of dueling pianos, this sports bar-jazz haunt has two grands set up facing each other on a raised stage (so, strictly speaking, it's 176 keys). The time to come is Friday or Saturday night, when two talented musicians belt out piano classics in unison (everything from Fats Domino to Billy Joel) with plenty of audience interaction. (☎206-839-1300; www.ilove88keys.com; 315 2nd Ave S; ☺5pm-2am; ☒Occidental Mall)

Pyramid Ale House CRAFT BEER

20 Map p44, C5

In SoDo by Safeco Field, this brewpub has the cleaned-up-industrial feel – all bricks and brass and designer lighting – that defines the Pacific Northwest brewpub. It's a nice mainstream (but still appreciably Seattle-ish) place to take your parents or tenderfoot visitors. But don't even try on a game day, unless you want to squeeze into the standing-room-only beer tent outdoors. (☎206-682-3377; www.pyramidbrew.com; 1201 1st Ave S; ☺11am-10pm Mon-Thu, 11am-11pm Fri & Sat, 11am-9pm Sun; ☒Stadium)

Caffè Umbria CAFE

21 Map p44, D3

Started by an Italian immigrant from Perugia, Umbria has a true Italian flavor with its 8oz cappuccinos, chatty clientele, pretty Italianate tiles and baguettes so fresh they must have been teleported over from Milan. Ideal for Italophiles and Starbucks-phobes. (☎206-624-5847; www.caffeumbria.com; 320 Occidental Ave S; ☺6am-6pm Mon-Fri, 7am-6pm Sat, 8am-5pm Sun; ☒Occidental Mall)

Entertainment

CenturyLink Field STADIUM

22 Map p44, D5

The late, mostly unlamented King-dome, long Seattle's biggest eyesore, was once the home field for the city's professional baseball and football franchises. Then it was imploded spectacularly in 2000 and replaced by this 72,000-seater stadium, home of the NFL's **Seattle Seahawks** (www.seahawks.com; tickets $42-95) and Seattle's soccer team, the **Sounders** (☎206-622-3415; www.seattlesounders.net; tickets from $37). (800 Occidental Ave S; ☒Stadium)

Safeco Field STADIUM

23 Map p44, D5

Home of Seattle's pro baseball team, the **Mariners** (www.mariners.org; tickets $7-60), the $517 million Safeco Field opened in July 1999. With its retractable roof, 47,000 seats and real grass,

 Top Tip

Sound of the Sounders

Sounders soccer fans are organized into half a dozen supporters groups and are famous for their highly musical 'March to the Match,' which kicks off from Occidental Park in Pioneer Sq (Map p44, C1) a good couple of hours before the real 'kick-off.' There's a 40-piece wind band, sporadic player appearances and lots of singing.

the stadium was funded by taxpayers and tourists, with the Mariners coughing up the difference. The stadium's unique design means it commands fantastic views of the surrounding mountains, downtown and Puget Sound. (☑206-346-4241; 1250 1st Ave S; tours adult/child $12/10; ⏱1¼hr tours 10:30am, 12:30pm & 2:30pm non-game days Apr-Oct; 🚇Stadium)

Nordo's Culinarium THEATER

24 Map p44, C3

A theatrical group with culinary inclinations, Cafe Nordo marries two themes in one – food and theater – putting on inspired play-cum-dinner shows where the performers double as the waitstaff. It's a unique formula first hatched in 2009 when the then homeless group put on occasional plays in Fremont's Theo Chocolate factory. (www.cafenordo.com; 109 S Main St; 🚇Occidental Mall)

Comedy Underground COMEDY

25 Map p44, C2

The best comedy club in Seattle has an 8:30pm show most nights and a second 10:30pm show on Fridays and Saturdays. Talent is mainly local and there's a full bar, plus a pizza-and-burger-style food menu. Under-21s are welcome Sunday to Thursday. Monday is open mike, a crapshoot of the surprisingly good or the skin-crawlingly bad. (☑206-628-0303; www.comedyunderground.com; 109 S Washington St; tickets $6-55; 🚇Occidental Mall)

Shopping

Filson SPORTS & OUTDOORS

26 Map p44, C5

Founded in 1897 as the original outfitters for prospectors heading for the Klondike, Filson is a long-standing Seattle legend that, in 2015, opened up this hugely impressive flagship store in SoDo. Wall-mounted bison heads and sepia-toned photos evoke the Klondike spirit while flop-down sofas and literary tomes encourage lingering. (☑206-622-3147; www.filson.com; 1741 1st Ave S; ⏱10am-6pm Mon-Sat, noon-5pm Sun; 🚇Stadium)

Globe Bookstore BOOKS

27 Map p44, C2

This small but comfortably cramped shop is an erudite emporium of new and secondhand books, not all of which make it on to the shelves. Thumbing through its piles and racks is so much more serendipitous than an online 'search.' (☑206-682-6882; 218 1st Ave S; ⏱10:30am-6pm; 🚇Occidental Mall)

Uwajimaya MALL

28 Map p44, F4

Founded by Fujimatsu Moriguchi, one of the few Japanese to return here from the WWII internment camps, this large department and grocery store – a cornerstone of Seattle's Asian community – has everything from fresh fish and exotic fruits and vegetables to cooking utensils, and you'll come face-to-face with those dim sum ingredients you've always wondered

about. (206-624-6248; www.uwajimaya.
com; 600 5th Ave S; 8am-10pm Mon-Sat,
9am-9pm Sun; 5th & Jackson/Japantown)

Flanagan & Lane Antiques ANTIQUES

29 Map p44, D3

This plush shop is devoted to American, English and Continental furniture
and myriad decorative pieces. It's good
if you're in the market for grandfather
clocks, or chairs and tables that look
as if they once accommodated French
royalty. (206-682-0098; www.flanagan-lane
antiques.com; 165 S Jackson St; 11am-5pm
Mon-Sat, noon-5pm Sun; Occidental Mall)

Glasshouse Studio ARTS & CRAFTS

30 Map p44, C3

The Seattle area is known for its
Pilchuck School of glassblowing art,
and Glasshouse is the city's oldest
glassblowing studio. Stop by to watch
the artists in action and pick up a
memento right at the source. (20
6-682-9939; 311 Occidental Ave S; demonstrations 10-11:30am & 1-5pm Mon-Sat;
Occidental Mall)

Cannabis City POT SHOP

31 Map p44, E5

Seattle's first licensed 'recreational'
pot shop opened in July 2014 to long
queues. Its first sale was apparently
to a 65-year-old grandmother. While
it doesn't look much from the outside,
the interior is rather plush with plenty of assistants to take you through
the basics. You'll need to show your
ID at the door. (206-682-1332; www.
cannabiscity.us; 2733 4th Ave S; 8am-9pm
Mon-Thu, 8am-10pm Fri, 9am-10pm Sat, 9am-
8pm Sun; SoDo)

Understand
The Original Skid Row

Recognized as a byword for decrepit urban neighborhoods everywhere, the
term 'skid row' originated in Seattle in the 1860s when greased logs were skid-
ded down First Hill to a timber mill on the shores of Elliott Bay owned by a local
lumber entrepreneur named Henry Yesler. The mill road – known officially as
Yesler Way but colloquially as Skid Row – was punctuated by a strip of bawdy
bars that grew up to support a rambunctious population of itinerant mill workers. Famed for its drunken revelry and fistfights, the area quickly acquired an
unsavory reputation, causing Seattle's affluent classes to migrate north to the
more salubrious streets of what is now the downtown core. Meanwhile, 'Skid
Row' was left to slip into a long decline, and an infamous nickname was born.

After decades of poverty, Yesler Way finally came out of its coma in the 1970s
after a vociferous community campaign saved the Pioneer Square Historic
District from the demolition ball.

Explore

Belltown & Seattle Center

Where industry once fumed, glassy condos now rise in the thin, walkable strip of Belltown. The neighborhood gained a reputation for trendsetting nightlife (read: grunge) in the 1990s, but these days it's more renowned for its 100-plus restaurants exhibiting a United Nations of flavors. The adjacent Seattle Center is anchored by the Space Needle, several iconic museums and endless entertainment possibilities.

The Sights in a Day

☀ Sometimes it's necessary to wake up to a doughnut and a cup of coffee. Exquisite examples of both can be procured at **Top Pot Hand-Forged Doughnuts** (p66). After the sweetening up, head over to Seattle Center for your first dose of fun. You can lose yourself for a good hour in **Chihuly Garden and Glass** (p58) and spend another one scanning the horizon from the top of the **Space Needle** (p56).

☀ It's worth popping back into Belltown for lunch. The **Macrina** (p66) bakery makes some of the best sandwiches in the city. Return to Seattle Center afterward where you can lose yourself in **MoPOP** (p60) for a couple of hours (more if you get stuck in the Sound Lab).

☾ Sunsets are lush framed by the outdoor art in the **Olympic Sculpture Park** (p66). With dark closing in, dive back into Belltown and choose your dinner flavor (from the myriad possibilities). Italian is always good in Seattle and the pasta at **Tavolàta** (p66) is impressively authentic.

For a local's day in Belltown, see p62.

◉ **Top Sights**

Space Needle (p56)

Chihuly Garden & Glass (p58)

Museum of Pop Culture (p60)

◯ **Local Life**

Belltown, Old & New (p62)

♥ **Best of Seattle**

Eating
Tavolàta (p66)

Top Pot Hand-Forged Doughnuts (p66)

Macrina (p66)

Serious Pie (p67)

Shiro's Sushi Restaurant (p67)

Live Music
Crocodile (p70)

Dimitriou's Jazz Alley (p63)

Seattle Opera (p71)

Tula's Jazz (p63)

Getting There

🚌 **Bus** Nearly all Belltown buses go up and down 3rd Ave and originate in downtown.

🚝 **Monorail** Running every 10 minutes between the Westlake Center and Seattle Center. Tickets cost $2.25/1 per adult/child. The journey takes two minutes.

Top Sights
Space Needle

Whether you're from Alabama or Timbuktu, your abiding image of Seattle will probably be of the Space Needle, a streamlined, modern-before-its-time tower built for the 1962 World's Fair that has been the city's defining symbol for over 50 years. The needle anchors the Seattle Center and persuades over a million annual visitors to ascend to its flying-saucer-like observation deck. Sure, it's crowded; but stop complaining and get in line: this is an essential Seattle pilgrimage.

👁 Map p64, C3

☎ 206-905-2100

www.spaceneedle.com

400 Broad St

adult/child $22/13

🕙 10am-9:30pm

🚇 Seattle Center

Admire it from the Outside

Standing apart from the rest of Seattle's skyscrapers, the Needle often looks taller than it actually is. On its completion in 1962, it was the highest structure west of the Mississippi River, topping 605ft, though it has since been easily surpassed (it's currently the seventh-tallest structure in Seattle).

Zip up the Elevators

The part of the Needle that's visible above ground weighs an astounding 3700 tons. Most visitors head for the 520ft-high observation deck on zippy elevators that ascend to the top in a mere 41 seconds. The 360-degree views of Seattle and its surrounding water and mountains are suitably fabulous.

Observation Deck

The observation deck has a cafe, copious wall-mounted facts, free telescopes and some interesting touch screens. One takes you on a 'virtual' walk through Pike Place Market, Seattle Aquarium and some of Lake Union's houseboats. Another is a high-powered telescope that you can move around and zoom in and out to see close-up images of the street below.

The Views

The alfresco part of the observation deck is guarded by a Perspex screen and an enclosed wire fence. The view is broad: on clear days, you can see three Cascade volcanoes (Mts Rainier, Baker and St Helens), the Olympic range, the jagged coastline of Puget Sound and the sparkling surfaces of Lakes Union and Washington fanning out in the haze.

☑ Top Tips

▶ There's a special day-and-night package (two separate entries) for $39. For a cheaper option, simply ascend half-an-hour before sunset and linger until it gets dark.

▶ There are a million ways to photograph the Space Needle in Seattle from locations all over town. Some favorites include: through one of the statues in the Olympic Sculpture Park (p66), or looking up from the Chihuly Garden (p58).

✗ Take a Break

If you decide to ascend the Space Needle, it's more economical to tie it in with lunch. Standard tickets cost $22. However, if you go up for lunch in the rotating **Sky-City Restaurant**, the standard entry will be waived as long as your order costs at least $25. The restaurant rotates fully every 47 minutes, ideal for a leisurely lunch. The menu is true to Seattle's locavore tradition with a strong emphasis on fish.

Top Sights
Chihuly Garden & Glass

Opened in 2012 and reinforcing Seattle's position as the Venice of North America, this exquisite exposition of the life and work of dynamic local sculptor Dale Chihuly is possibly the finest collection of curated glass art you'll ever see. It shows off Chihuly's creative designs in a suite of interconnected dark and light rooms, before depositing you in an airy glass atrium and – finally – a landscaped garden in the shadow of the Space Needle.

Map p64, B3

206-753-4940

www.chihulygardenand glass.com

305 Harrison St

adult/child $27/16

11am-6pm Sun-Thurs, till 7pm Fri & Sat

Seattle Center

Sealife Tower

The first standout exhibit in the Exhibition Hall is Sealife Tower, a huge azure structure of intricately blown glass that looks as if it has sprung straight out of Poseidon's lair. Look out for the small octopuses and starfish melded into the swirling waves and examine Chihuly's early sketches for the works that adorn the surrounding walls.

Ikebana & Float Boat

The Ikebana & Float Boat consists of several boats overflowing with round glass balls and was inspired by Chihuly's time in Venice: he casually threw luminous glass spheres into the canals and watched as local children enthusiastically collected them in boats.

The Glasshouse

Sitting like a giant greenhouse under the Space Needle, the Glasshouse offers a nod to London's erstwhile Crystal Palace, one of Chihuly's historical inspirations. You'll notice that the floor space of the Glasshouse has been left empty, drawing your eye up to the ceiling where a huge medley of flower-shaped glass pieces imitate the reds, oranges and yellows of a perfect sunset.

The Garden

Chihuly uses the garden to demonstrate the seamless melding of glass art and natural vegetation. Many of the alfresco pieces are simple pointed shards of glass reminiscent of luminescent reeds, but the real eye-catcher is **The Sun**, a riot of twisted yellow 'flames' whose swirling brilliance erases the heaviness of the most overcast Seattle sky.

☑ **Top Tips**

▶ Use your Chihuly inspiration to make your own glass art at the nearby **Seattle Glassblowing Studio** (www.seattleglassblowing. com; 2227 5th Ave; ◔9am-6pm Mon-Sat, 10am-6pm Sun; ◻13) in Belltown.

▶ You can run an audio tour on your cell phone while viewing the exhibits. Simply download it from the museum website.

✗ **Take A Break**

The best place to get refreshments is in the museum's **Collections Cafe**, an art exhibit in itself, where you can get everything from a burger to king salmon. For cheap fast food, pop across to the adjacent Seattle Center Armory and its food court.

Top Sights
Museum of Pop Culture

The Museum of Pop Culture (MoPOP) is an inspired marriage between super-modern architecture and legendary rock-and-roll history that sprang from the imagination (and pocket) of Microsoft co-creator Paul Allen. Inside its avant-garde frame, designed by Canadian architect Frank Gehry, you can tune into the famous sounds of Seattle, including Jimi Hendrix and grunge, or attempt to imitate the rock masters in an Interactive 'Sound Lab.' There's a permanent science-fiction exhibit encased in the same dramatic building.

Map p64, C3

206-770-2700

www.mopop.org

325 5th Ave N

adult/child $25/16

10am-7pm Jun-Aug, to 5pm Sep-May

Seattle Center

Architecture

The highly unusual building with its crinkled folds colored in metallic blues and purples was designed by renowned Canadian architect Frank Gehry, a strong proponent of deconstructivism. Gehry – who designed the equally outlandish Guggenheim Museum in Bilbao – supposedly used one of Hendrix's smashed-up guitars as his inspiration.

Main Exhibits

The main exhibit hall is anchored by *If VI Was IX*, a tower of 700 instruments, designed by German-born artist Trimpin. Many of the permanent exhibits center on Hendrix, including the Fender Stratocaster guitar that he played at Woodstock in 1969. There's also a nostalgic slice of grunge memorabilia in a section entitled *Nirvana: Taking Punk to the Masses*.

Sound Lab

Most of the 3rd floor is given over to the interactive Sound Lab, where you can lay down vocal tracks, play instruments, fiddle with effects pedals and – best of all – jam in several mini studios. **On Stage** takes things further, allowing you the opportunity to belt out numbers under stage lights with a virtual audience.

Icons of Science Fiction

A separate Science Fiction Museum opened on the site in 2004 and, in 2012, was incorporated into MoPOP in a permanent 2nd-floor minimuseum called Icons of Science Fiction, which displays artifacts from iconic films and TV shows. Expect to come face to face with a *Doctor Who* Dalek and plenty of *Star Wars* life forms and film props.

☑ Top Tips

▸ Save up to $3 by booking online.

▸ Entry to the 'Icons of Science Fiction' costs $3 extra – a sound investment.

▸ Tickets last all day, meaning you can leave the complex and re-enter.

▸ For a great photo, try catching the Space Needle reflected on MoPOP's purple-blue metallic walls.

✕ Take a Break

MoPOP has its own bar-cafe, appropriately called Pop Kitchen & Bar, that sells reasonably priced appetite-killers – including sandwiches, burgers and pizzas – along with a good range of local microbrews. Another eating option is the adjacent Seattle Center Armory, which sports a food court full of familiar franchises on its ground floor.

Local Life
Belltown, Old & New

Belltown is a rapidly changing neighborhood that has both its detractors and its fans. The former lament the days when bolshie bars outnumbered cocktail lounges and if you stage-dived an adoring crowd would catch you. The latter claim that, gentrification aside, Belltown is still a rambunctious quarter chock-a-block with bars, restaurants and music venues; it's just the demographic that's altered.

❶ The Moore

There are various reasons why you should start this dip into Belltown's local life at the **Moore** (www.moorehotel.com; 1926 2nd Ave; ☒Westlake) aside from its economical hotel. Not only does it possess a great little shoulder-to-shoulder coffee shop; it also harbors one of Belltown's last true dives, the **Nitelite Lounge** (✆206-443-0899; ⏱4pm-2am;), and the

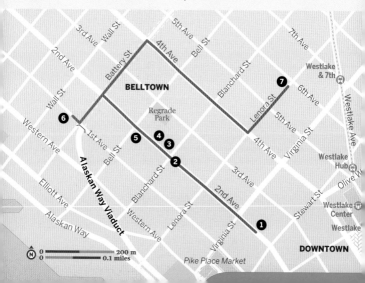

oldest theater in Seattle, all in one massive building.

❷ Second Ave Bars

The tight cluster of bars and clubs on the stretch of 2nd Ave between Battery and Blanchard Sts is about all that's left of ungentrified Belltown. Jump into the nocturnal melee before it's too late.

❸ Tula's Jazz

Not a lot of people know it, but Seattle was a hive of jazzy creativity in the 1940s and '50s. Some of the legacy remains, at least in Belltown where **Dimitriou's Jazz Alley** (p70) books national and international jazz acts. For a slice of the contemporary scene, however, you'll need to hit the more intimate **Tula's Jazz** (☑206-443-4221; www.tulas.com; 2214 2nd Ave; ⏰4pm-midnight; ☐13) on boozy 2nd Ave.

❹ Lava Lounge

With its well-worn, tiki-themed decor, games of all kinds and over-the-top art on the walls, the **Lava Lounge** (☑206-441-5660; 2226 2nd Ave; ⏰3pm-2am; ☐13) is more old-school Belltown than new. The cocktail bar sits on an agreeably disheveled block of 2nd Ave also inhabited by a handful of other much-loved dives.

❺ Bedlam

There's nothing mad about **Bedlam** (www.bedlamite.com; 2231 2nd Ave; ⏰6am-10pm Mon-Fri, 7am-10pm Sat & Sun; ☐13),

unless you count the wall-mounted bicycle and the Space Needle sculpture – made out of old junk – that guards the door. Welcome to a one-off coffee bar with no pretensions and a low geek count that specializes in decent lattes and ultra-thick slices of wholemeal toast loaded with peanut butter and jam.

❻ Cyclops

Sometimes when you're tramping the streets in search of food and drink (and a bathroom) after a day of arduous sightseeing, all you want is somewhere cheap, unpretentious and comfortable to rest your weary legs. Welcome to **Cyclops** (www.cyclopsseattle.com; 2421 1st Ave; mains from $8; ⏰5pm-2am daily, 9am-2pm Sat & Sun; ☐13), where a pint of Boundary Bay IPA and a good ole' burger can be consumed amid the to-ing and fro-ing of Belltown life.

❼ Assembly Hall

Part of the new Belltown that has made noble attempts to incorporate the old, the **Assembly Hall** (☑206-812-8413; www.assemblyhallseattle.com; 2121 6th Ave; sandwiches $8-9; ⏰6am-6pm Mon-Fri, 7am-6pm Sat & Sun; ☐Westlake & 7th) is a food and drink emporium run by star Seattle restaurateur Tom Douglas. It harbors a cafe, a brunch spot, a farm-fresh food market and – best of all – a mezzanine floor full of free games, including pool and shuffle board. A great social leveler.

200 m
0.1 miles

For reviews see

⊙	Top Sights	p56
⊙	Sights	p66
✕	Eating	p66
🍷	Drinking	p70
✿	Entertainment	p70

N Aurora Ave N

Denny Way

Denny Way

John St

6th Ave N

Thomas St

Harrison St

Taylor Ave N

Mercer St

5th Ave N

5th Ave N

4th Ave N

4th Ave N

Broad St

John St

Museum of Pop Culture

Memorial Stadium

Seattle Center

Space Needle

Chihuly Garden & Glass

Pacific Science Center

SEATTLE CENTER

Seattle Center House/ Children's Museum

Denny Way

2nd Ave N

Mercer St

Seattle Repertory Theatre

Warren Ave N

Warren Ave N

Key Arena

Republican St

Thomas St

John St

1st Ave N

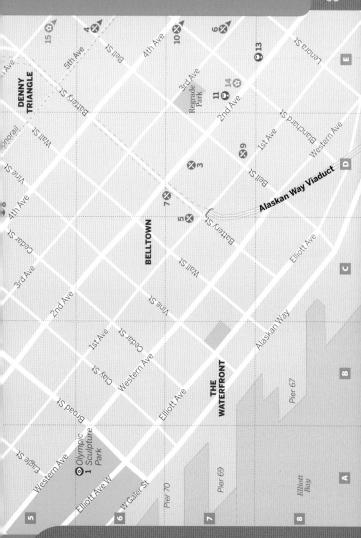

DENNY
TRIANGLE

15

4

Bell St

5th Ave

4th Ave

10

6

13

3rd Ave
Battery St

Regrade
Park

11

14

2nd Ave

1st Ave

Blanchard St

Lenora St

Western Ave

Wall St

Vine St

4th Ave

9

Bell St

7

5

Battery St

Alaskan Way Viaduct

BELLTOWN

Cedar St

3rd Ave

Wall St

Vine St

Elliott Ave

2nd Ave

Cedar St

Vine St

Alaskan Way

1st Ave

Western Ave

Elliott Ave

THE
WATERFRONT

Pier 67

Clay St

Broad St

Eagle St

Western Ave

Olympic
1 Sculpture
Park

Elliott Ave W

W Galer St

Pier 70

Pier 69

Pier 67

Elliott
Bay

E

D

C

B

A

5

6

7

8

Sights

Olympic Sculpture Park
PARK, SCULPTURE

1 Map p64, A6

This smart urban renewal project and outpost of the Seattle Art Museum was inaugurated in 2007 to widespread local approval. The terraced park is landscaped over railway tracks and overlooks Puget Sound with the distant Olympic Mountains winking on the horizon. Joggers and dog-walkers meander daily through its zigzagging paths, enjoying over 20 pieces of modern sculpture. (2901 Western Ave; admission free; ⏱sunrise-sunset; 📖13)

Pacific Science Center
MUSEUM

2 ◉ Map p64, B4

This interactive museum of science and industry once housed the science pavilion of the 1962 World's Fair. Today the center features virtual-reality exhibits, a tropical butterfly house, laser shows, holograms and other wonders of science, many with hands-on demonstrations. Also on the premises is the vaulted-screen **IMAX Theater**, a saltwater tide pool and a planetarium. (📞206-443-2001; www.pacificsciencecenter.org; 200 2nd Ave N; adult/child exhibits only $19.75/14.75, with IMAX $25.75/18.75; ⏱10am-5pm Mon-Fri, 10am-6pm Sat & Sun; 👶; 📖Seattle Center)

Eating

Tavolàta
ITALIAN $$

3 🍴 Map p64, D7

Owned by top Seattle chef Ethan Stowell, Tavolàta is a dinner-only Italian-inspired eatery emphasizing homemade pasta dishes. Keeping things simple with venison-stuffed ravioli and linguine nero (clams with black pasta), the results are as good as those found in Italy – and there's no praise finer than that! (📞206-838-8008; 2323 2nd Ave; pasta dishes $18-22; ⏱5-11pm; 📖13)

Top Pot Hand-Forged Doughnuts
CAFE $

4 🍴 Map p64, E6

Sitting pretty in a glass-fronted former car showroom with art-deco signage and immense bookshelves, Top Pot's flagship cafe produces the Ferraris of the doughnut world. It might have morphed into a 20-outlet chain in recent years, but its hand-molded collection of sweet rings are still – arguably – worth visiting Seattle for alone. The coffee's pretty potent too. (www.toppotdoughnuts.com; 2124 5th Ave; doughnuts from $1.50; ⏱6am-7pm Mon-Fri, 7am-7pm Sat & Sun; 📖13)

Macrina
BAKERY $

5 🍴 Map p64, C7

That snaking queue out the door is there for a reason: damned good

Olympic Sculpture Park

artisan bread (you can watch through the window as the experts roll out the dough). There are two options and two lines at Macrina. One is for the fantastic take-out bakery (possibly the best in Seattle); the other's for the sit-down cafe with its so-good-it-could-be-Paris sandwiches, soups and other such snacks. Join the pilgrimage. (☎206-448-4032; www.macrinabakery. com; 2408 1st Ave; sandwiches $5-8.75; ⊙7am-6pm; ☒13)

Serious Pie
PIZZA $$

6 ✖ Map p64, E7

In the crowded confines of Serious Pie you can enjoy beautifully blistered pizza bases topped with such unconventional ingredients as clams, potatoes, nettles, soft eggs, truffle cheese and more. Be prepared to share a table and meet a few Seattleites. The pizzas have proved so popular that Serious Pie has spawned several new outlets, including one in the Starbucks Reserve Roastery. (☎206-838-7388; www.tomdouglas.com; 316 Virginia St; pizzas $16-18; ⊙11am-11pm; ☒Westlake)

Shiro's Sushi Restaurant
JAPANESE $$

7 ✖ Map p64, D7

A little on the pricey side, but with over 20 years of glowing testimonies about its black cod and deep-fried

Understand

It Happened at the World's Fair

Known officially as the Century 21 Exposition, Seattle's 1962 World's Fair set out to depict the future, as envisaged through the eyes of an affluent Cold War generation still trapped in the rigid social mores of the 1950s. Looking back today, many of its exhibits look like relics from a Flash Gordon movie, although the expo's larger infrastructure has endured, most notably the monorail (an early experiment in mass transit that was way ahead of its time), the Space Needle (p56) – a distinctive city icon – and the Pacific Science Center (p66).

Elvis Makes an Appearance

Running for six months between April and October 1962, the fair attracted 10 million visitors, including a freshly demobbed Elvis Presley in the throes of a skin-crawlingly trite movie career. *It Happened at the World's Fair* was partly filmed in Seattle, and Presley's presence caused quite a stir – although not with the critics, who called the movie a lemon. The fair itself garnered more plaudits and turned a tidy profit (unusual for the time). It also helped cement Seattle as a top-tier American city.

A View of the Future

Overshadowed by the Cold War, the fair's main themes were science, the future and 'outer space' (President Kennedy famously pledged to put a man on the moon, in a speech made in September 1962 while the fair was still running). The World of Science exhibit hosted a fantastical Spacearium that took visitors on a virtual journey to the outer galaxies, while the World of Tomorrow sported a Bubbleator: a hydraulic elevator that lifted visitors through a series of aluminum cubes and foretold the future. For all its playful predictions, Century 21 was more an end than a beginning. It closed under the shadow of the Cuban Missile Crisis with Kennedy crying off the closing ceremony to deal with more urgent affairs (ie possible nuclear annihilation). In little over a year, the president would be dead, US soldiers would be dispatched to Vietnam and America would be taking off its '50s straitjacket and embracing the hippy-dippy 1960s.

prawn heads, Shiro's is Belltown's best Japanese option. Although founder Shiro Kashiba no longer runs the restaurant, it has kept its name and reputation for cool, sophisticated food and service. (☑206-443-9844; www. shiros.com; 2401 2nd Ave; 5-piece sashimi $14-20; ⏱5-10pm; ☐13)

Tilikum
Place Cafe   BISTRO, BRUNCH $$

8 Map p64, D5

Sometimes old Belltown and new Belltown sit bumper to bumper, and the juxtaposition is never more marked than on Cedar St, where the suave, pseudo-Parisian Tilikum Place Cafe lies next door to 90-year-old dive bar, the Five Point Café. The former has the words 'European bistro' written all over it and is particularly popular for lunch (quiche, sardine sandwiches) and brunch (baked pancakes). (☑206-282-4830; www. tilikumplacecafe.com; 407 Cedar St; brunch mains $9-14; ⏱11am-10pm Mon-Fri, 8am-10pm Sat & Sun; ☐3)

360 Local   NORTHWEST $$

9 Map p64, D7

Snaring 90% of its ingredients from within a 360-mile radius, this restaurant follows its ambitious 'locavore' manifesto pretty rigidly. The farms where your meat was reared are displayed on the daily blackboard menu and the restaurant's wood-finish interior looks like a rustic barn. With such a fertile hinterland to draw upon, the food is pretty special; try the rabbit, the clams or the chickpea cake. (☑20 6-441-9360; www.local360.org; cnr 1st Ave & Bell St; mains $14-28; ⏱11am-late Mon-Fri, 9am-late Sat & Sun; ☐13)

Dahlia Lounge   NORTHWESTERN $$$

10 Map p64, E7

Seattle's most well-known and decorated chef, Tom Douglas, established his rapidly growing restaurant empire here in 1989. Some say it has single-handedly made Seattleites more sophisticated with its now familiar Douglas hallmarks: locally-grown produce, organic ethos and fusion flavors that lean heavily toward Pacific Northwestern favorites. The seasonal spot prawns and Dungeness crab cakes are standout dishes. (☑20 6-682-4142; www.tomdouglas.com; 2001 4th Ave; mains $26-38; ⏱11:30am-2:30pm & 5-10pm Mon-Fri, 9am-2pm & 5-11pm Sat & Sun; ☐Westlake)

Local Life
Myrtle Edwards Park

Your best bet for an uninterrupted walk, jog or cycle if you're staying downtown is **Myrtle Edwards Park** (☐13), a favorite of joggers and power-walkers pursuing lunchtime fitness. In warm weather the linked paths, with stupendous views over the Sound to the Olympic Mountains, make a good place for a picnic. It's adjacent to the Olympic Sculpture Park (p66).

Drinking

Shorty's
BAR

11 Map p64, E7

Shorty's is all about beer, arcade games and music (mostly punk and metal). A remnant of Belltown's grungier days that refuses to become an anachronism, it keeps the lights low and the music loud. Pinball machines are built into some of the tables, and basic snacks (hot dogs, nachos) soak up the booze. (206-441-5449; www.shortydog.com; 2222 2nd Ave; noon-2am; 13)

Five Point Café
BAR

12 Map p64, D5

There are Belltown relics and then there's the Five Point, whose seedy neon sign and cantankerous advertising blurb ('cheating tourists and drunks since 1929') is practically as iconic as the Space Needle – and 33 years older! Half diner, half bar and far too worn-in to be mistaken for hip, it's a spot where seasoned Charles Bukowski look-a-likes go to get wasted, any time of day. (206-448-9993; www.the5pointcafe.com; 415 Cedar St; 24hr; 3)

The Whisky Bar
BAR

13 Map p64, E8

This recently reopened bar, relocated a block or so from its old haunt, is about more than just the whiskey, though that, of course, is good. If you're sticking to home turf, try the locally-made Westland single malt. There are genuine British food treats on offer as well. Where else in Seattle can you get Welsh rarebit – or Scotch eggs for that matter? (206-443-4490; www.thewhiskybar.com; 2122 2nd Ave; 2pm-2am Mon-Fri, noon-2am Sat & Sun; 13)

Entertainment

Crocodile
LIVE MUSIC

14 Map p64, E7

Nearly old enough to be called a Seattle institution, the Crocodile is a clamorous 560-capacity music venue that first opened in 1991, just in time to grab the coattails of the grunge explosion. Everyone who's anyone in Seattle's alt-music scene has since played here, including a famous occasion in 1992 when Nirvana appeared unannounced supporting Mudhoney. (206-441-4618; www.thecrocodile.com; 2200 2nd Ave; 13)

Dimitriou's Jazz Alley
JAZZ

15 Map p64, E5

Hidden in quite an unlikely spot behind a boring-looking office building is Seattle's most sophisticated and prestigious jazz club. Dimitriou's plays host to the best of the locals as well as many national and international acts passing through. (206-441-9729; www.jazzalley.com; 2033 6th Ave; shows 7:30pm & 9:30pm; Westlake & 7th)

Myrtle Edwards Park (p69)

Seattle Opera
OPERA

16 ⭐ Map p64, C1

Seattle Opera is distinguished and diverse. Based at the **McCaw Hall** (📞206-684-7200; 321 Mercer St), it has hosted everything from Verdi's *La Traviata* to Pete Townshend's *Tommy*. It's particularly known for its performances of Wagner's *Ring* cycle, first staged in 1973. (www.seattleopera.org; 🚇Seattle Center)

Seattle Children's Theater
THEATER

17 ⭐ Map p64, B3

This highly esteemed theater group has two auditoriums in its Seattle Center campus. Friday and Saturday matinees and evening performances run September to June. There's also a Drama School summer season. (📞206-441-3322; www.sct.org; 201 Thomas St; tickets $27-40; ⊙Thu-Sun Sep-Jun; 🚇Seattle Center)

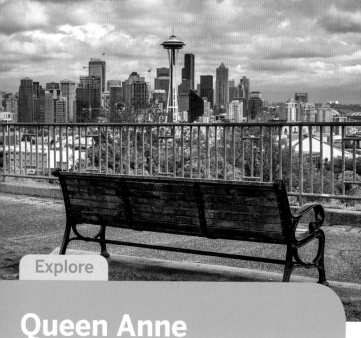

Explore

Queen Anne & Lake Union

Salubrious Queen Anne hoards old money in beautiful fin-de-siècle mansions that sit stacked on a hill. Down below lies sparkling Lake Union dominated by SLU (South Lake Union), a fast evolving neighborhood that is changing faster than the fresh-faced influx of techies can tweet about it, with clean-lined restaurants, a congestion-easing streetcar and the sprawling campus of Amazon.com.

The Sights in a Day

☀️ Get biscuits for breakfast in **Serious Biscuit** (p83), one of over a dozen stalwart businesses owned by Seattle culinary phenomenon, Tom Douglas, before heading over to the lakeshore to wise up on the more engaging aspects of Seattle's past in the **Museum of History & Industry** (p74).

☀️ Dive back into the SLU for a light Italian lunch at **Caffè Torino** (p82). Return to Lake Union Park and while away the afternoon on a sailboat trip organized at the **Center for Wooden Boats** (p80).

🌙 Climb Queen Anne's steep **Counterbalance** (p76) while it's still light and admire the opulent mansions on Highland Dr before stopping at **Kerry Park** (p80) for the best views of the city. It's all downhill to Lower Queen Anne and a dinner appointment at Cajun food haven, **Toulouse Petit** (p81).

For a local's day in Queen Anne, see p76.

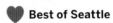

👁 Top Sights

Museum of History & Industry (p74)

🔍 Local Life

Queen Anne Coffee Crawl (p76)

💜 Best of Seattle

Coffee Spots

El Diablo Coffee Co (p77)

Caffè Torino (p82)

Caffè Ladro (p77)

Caffè Fiore (p77)

Shopping

REI (p85)

Queen Anne Book Company (p85)

Getting There

🚌 **Bus** Metro buses 2 and 13 run frequently to Queen Anne from downtown and Seattle Center. Buses 62 and 70 serve the Westlake and Eastlake neighborhoods of Lake Union from downtown.

🚋 **Tram** One of Seattle's two main streetcar lines runs between South Lake Union and the Westlake Center in downtown every 10 minutes.

Top Sights
Museum of History & Industry

Almost everything you need to know about Seattle is crammed into the fabulous Museum of History & Industry (MOHAI), located in plush digs on the southern shore of Lake Union. In operation since the 1950s, and with an archive of over four million objects, MOHAI displays its stash of historical booty in an impressively repurposed naval armory building. If only school history lessons could've been this riveting.

Map p78, F3

206-324-1126

www.mohai.org

860 Terry Ave N

adult/child under 14yr $19.95/free

10am-5pm, 10am-8pm 1st Thu of month

Lake Union Park

Boeing Airplane

The big eye-catcher as you walk into the huge hangar-sized space is a 1919 Boeing airplane hanging from the roof (the first commercial Boeing ever made). Indeed, the name Boeing looms large over the whole museum, along with numerous other Seattle icons (Starbucks, Rainier beer, grunge).

Interactive Exhibits

In Microsoft city, there is no shortage of interactive exhibits to enjoy, including a photo and comment booth, touchscreen TVs and an opportunity to explore railroad history by banging large mallets on railway sleepers. With so many artifacts to call upon exhibits can change regularly, although the museum's overriding sentiment is an unashamed celebration of Seattle's action-packed history.

The Upper Floors

On the upper floors rooms are arranged around a mezzanine with the exhibits unfolding chronologically using various themes to paint a multi-layered portrait of the city, room by room. Highlights include the early Native American settlers, the 1889 Great Fire, the 1962 World's Fair and a focus on film and TV covering everything from *Twin Peaks* to *Grey's Anatomy*.

Films & Temporary Shows

A short but attention-grabbing film in a purpose-built theater on level two advertises Seattle in all its scenic and musical splendor. Regularly changing temporary shows are also a feature in a suite of rooms nearby; a recent hit was 'The Legacy of Seattle Hip-Hop'.

☑ **Top Tips**

▶ The museum offers free entry on the first Thursday of every month between 10am and 8pm.

▶ Ditch the car (SLU is notorious for road-works); outside the museum there's a tram stop (10 minutes to downtown), a bike-share docking station, or – if you're intrepid – a boat moorage.

✕ **Take a Break**

The museum has its own MOHAI Cafe; good for lunch or a snack. Otherwise, various Seattle coffee chainlets such as Top Pot Hand-Forged Doughnuts and Uptown Espresso (525 Queen Anne Ave N) lurk in South Lake Union's dense grid.

Look out for food carts here as well, especially around lunchtime on weekdays.

Local Life
Queen Anne Coffee Crawl

Queen Anne is a microcosm of Seattle's famously fertile coffee scene. It's not coincidental that quite a few of the city's coffee chains opened up their first cafes here. To experience the best of the best in caffeine-infused drinks and mingle among coffee-addicted locals with discerning palates, head out of Belltown on Queen Anne Ave N and keep walking.

1 Lower Queen Anne
Hungry tourists from the Seattle Center bump into affluent young techies on their lunch breaks in Lower Queen Anne, or Uptown as it's sometimes known, the thin strip at the bottom of the **Counterbalance** (p80) that strikes a less haughty pose than its eponymous neighbor up on the hill. Uptown is locally renowned for its

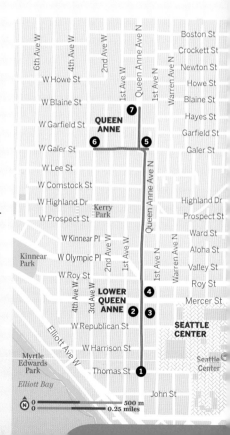

eclectic mix of economical restaurants and coffee shops.

❷ Uptown Espresso

Examine the velvet foam on your latte at **Uptown Espresso Bar** (☎206-285-3757; 525 Queen Anne Ave N; ⊙5am-10pm Mon-Thu, 5am-11pm Fri, 6am-11pm Sat, 6am-10pm Sun; 🗟; 🚍13) while eavesdropping on cell-phone conversations, yoga enthusiasts comparing breathing techniques, and 20-somethings bragging about how many Twitter followers they have. The business was founded in the '80s but, unlike Starbucks, it has remained a purely Seattle institution.

❸ Mecca Cafe

You can choose your poison – caffeine or alcohol – in **Mecca Café** (☎206-285-9728; 526 Queen Anne Ave N; burgers $8.75; ⊙7am-2am; 🚍13), Lower Queen Anne's dive bar of choice. Half of the long, skinny room is a ketchup-on-the-table diner, the other side is a slam-it-down bar where the beer mats are as tattooed as the customers. Opened at the tail-end of prohibition, it's been a reliable spreader of local gossip since 1930.

❹ Caffe Ladro

After Mecca, **Ladro** (www.caffeladro.com; 2205 Queen Anne Ave N; ⊙5:30am-8pm Sun-Thu, 5:30am-9pm Fri & Sat; 🗟; 🚍13) is positively refined. The Seattle-only coffee chain now has 15 branches and not only does it roast its own beans, it also bakes its own pastries. For a double whammy of bitter and sweet, place your order in the cozy corner cafe and give yourself enough rocket fuel to climb the Counterbalance, the steep hill that starts just outside the door.

❺ 5 Spot

If you're coming from the city center on foot, you'll have earned breakfast by the time you hit **5 Spot** (www.chowfoods. com; 1502 Queen Anne Ave N; brunch $8-14; ⊙8am-11pm Mon-Fri, 8am-3pm & 5pm-midnight Sat & Sun; 🖐; 🚍2) perched on top of the Counterbalance. Tired feet or not, expect a queue. The place is perennially popular for its weekend brunches with reviving cups of coffee on the side.

❻ Caffè Fiore

You're more likely to detect the aroma of coffee than *fiore* (flowers) in this tucked-away neighborhood staple, one of several Seattle coffee chainlets that opened their first **cafe** (☎206-282-1441; www.caffefiore.com; 224 W Galer St; ⊙6am-6pm Mon-Sat, 7am-6pm Sun; 🗟🖐; 🚍2) in Queen Anne. The flavor of choice? Locals rave about the Sevilla – a mocha with orange zest – but the espressos are pretty potent, too.

❼ El Diablo Coffee Co

If you're an expat Cuban, visiting Cubaphile, or are just sick of Seattle's default lattes, try a *café cubano* (a sweetened double espresso) at **El Diablo Coffee Co** (www.eldiablocoffee. com; 1811 Queen Anne Ave N; ⊙5:30am-8pm Mon-Fri, 6:30am-8pm Sat, 6:30am-6pm Sun; 🗟; 🚍13), Queen Anne's little piece of Caribbean heaven. They serve excellent rice and beans, too.

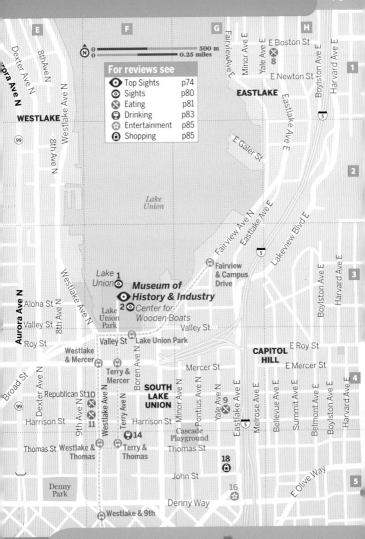

EASTLAKE

E Boston St

E Newton St

For reviews see
⚫ Top Sights	p74
⊙ Sights	p80
✕ Eating	p81
🍷 Drinking	p83
✪ Entertainment	p85
🅐 Shopping	p85

WESTLAKE

Lake
Union

500 m
0.25 miles

Lake
Union

**Museum of
History & Industry**

2 Center for
Wooden Boats

Fairview
& Campus
Drive

**CAPITOL
HILL**

E Roy St

E Mercer St

Valley St

Lake Union Park

Westlake
& Mercer

Terry &
Mercer

Republican St 10

**SOUTH
LAKE
UNION**

Mercer St

Harrison St

Thomas St Westlake &
Thomas

Terry &
Thomas

14

Cascade
Playground

Thomas St

18
🅐

Denny
Park

John St

16
✪

Denny Way

Westlake & 9th

E Olive Way

Sights

Lake Union
LAKE

1 Map p78, F3

Unifying Seattle's various bodies of water, freshwater Lake Union was carved by glacial erosion 12,000 years ago. Native American Duwamish tribes once subsisted on its then-isolated shores, but 21st-century Lake Union is backed by densely packed urban neighborhoods and is linked to both Lake Washington and Puget Sound by the Lake Washington Ship Canal (built as part of a huge engineering project in the 1910s). (🚏Lake Union Park)

Center for Wooden Boats
MUSEUM

2 Map p78, F3

Honoring Seattle's historical, aquatic and Native American antecedents, this one-of-a-kind museum and enthusiasts' center features vintage and replica boats and offers sailing lessons, including an excellent beginner course that gives you eight to 12 lessons over a four-month period. Best of all, however, are its free Sunday public sailboat rides on Lake Union (first come, first served; sign-ups start at 10am). (📞206-382-2628; www.cwb.org; 1010 Valley St; sailboat/rowboat rental per hr $38/35, beginner sailing course $420; ⏱10am-6pm Tue-Sun; ♿; 🚏Lake Union Park)

Kerry Park
PARK, VIEWPOINT

3 Map p78, B3

Amid the glittering Beverly Hills-like mansions of Highland Dr, mere commoners can enjoy eagle-eye views of downtown Seattle and Elliott Bay (and Mt Rainier, should it take the cloudy hat off) from this spectacular lookout. (211 W Highland Dr; ♿; 🚌2)

Queen Anne Counterbalance
AREA

4 Map p78, C3

The streetcar that chugged up and down the steep grade along Queen Anne Ave started operating on overhead-wire electricity in 1900, but it still needed some help to manage the hill. So engineers designed a system of counterweights – a 16-ton train that ran in a tunnel under the street would go up when the cable car went down and vice versa. The cable cars were retired in 1943, but the underground tunnels are still

---

Local Life
Cheshiahud Loop

Circumnavigating Lake Union, the **Cheshiahud Loop** (Map p78, F3) is a well-signposted six-mile amalgam of paths and sidewalks liberally used by local walkers, joggers and cyclists. It's good for lake vistas, people-watching and admiring Seattle's famous houseboats. Join the trail in Lake Union Park next to the Museum of History & Industry (p74).

Center for Wooden Boats

there (although they're not currently open to the public). (Queen Anne Ave N, north of W Roy St; 2)

Eating

Toulouse Petit   CAJUN, CREOLE $$

5 Map p78, B4

Hailed for its generous happy hours, cheap brunches and rollicking atmosphere, this perennially busy Queen Anne eatery has the common touch. The menu is large and varied, offering choices such as blackened rib-eye steak, freshwater gulf prawns and house-made gnocchi with artichoke hearts. (☑206-432-9069; www. toulousepetit.com; 601 Queen Anne Ave N; mains $19-26; ◷8am-2am; ☐13)

Canlis   AMERICAN $$$

6 ☒ Map p78, D1

One of Seattle's most celebrated restaurants, Canlis is old-school posh and one of the few places in the city where people regularly get dressed up for dinner. The menu is Pacific Northwest traditional (halibut, pork, fresh veg and Grand Marnier soufflé) and the decor's like something out of a 1950s-era Hitchcock movie – all angled glass and sweeping views. (☑206-283-3313; 2576 Aurora Ave N; 3-/4-course dinner $85/100; ◷5:30pm-late Mon-Sat; ☐5)

TODD PEARSON/GETTY IMAGES ©

Kayakers on Lake Union

regional Tuscan-style cooking, with simply prepared meat and fish, as well as pastas that can be ordered as a first or main course. A gorgeous leafy deck area behind the restaurant doubles as the entryway to **Cicchetti**, Serafina's sister restaurant, which serves Mediterranean snacks. Reservations are recommended. (📞206-323-0807; www.serafinaseattle.com; 2043 Eastlake Ave E; starters $5-12, pastas $16-18, mains $23-42; ⏱11:30am-2:30pm & 5-10pm Mon-Fri, 5-11pm Sat, 10am-2:30pm & 5-11pm Sun; 🚌70)

Caffè Torino
ITALIAN, SANDWICHES $

9 Map p78, G4

If you're up on the nuances of regional Italian food culture, you'll know that Turin (Torino) is a temple of good food and coffee, which is why you may want to decamp here for a Lavazza cappuccino, a Nutella cookie and a Caprese sandwich. Best of all is Caffè Torino's honoring of the *aperitivo* tradition, the late-afternoon *pausa* for cheap bites and prosecco. (📞206-682-2099; www.caffetorinoseattle.com; 422 Yale Ave N; sandwiches $7-8.50; ⏱6:30am-6pm Mon-Fri, 8am-5pm Sat & Sun; 🛜; 🚌Terry & Mercer)

Peso's Kitchen & Lounge
MEXICAN, BREAKFAST $$

A place that wears many sombreros, Peso's (see 5 Map p78, B4) serves fine Mexican food in the evenings amid a cool, trendy scene that is anything but Mexican. But the trump card comes the next morning, after the beautiful people have gone home, with an acclaimed egg-biased

How to Cook a Wolf
ITALIAN $$

7 Map p78, C1

Despite its scary name, the Ethan Stowell-run HTCAW has nothing to do with roasting wild fauna over your campfire. Rather the name is poached from a book written by MFK Fisher during wartime rationing about how to make the most of limited ingredients. Though times have changed, Stowell embraces the same philosophy. (📞206-838-8090; www.ethanstowellrestaurants.com; 2208 Queen Anne Ave N; pasta $16-19; ⏱5-11pm; 🚌13)

Serafina
ITALIAN $$

8 Map p78, H1

This lovely neighborhood Italian restaurant in Eastlake specializes in

breakfast. (📞206-283-9353; www.
pesoskitchenandlounge.com; 605 Queen
Anne Ave N; brunch $9-15, dinner $12-17;
🕓4pm-midnight Mon & Tue, 11am-2am Wed
& Thu, 9am-2am Fri-Sun; 🚌13)

Re:public
MODERN AMERICAN **$$**

10 Map p78, F4

Although the name might read like the
sobriquet of a rap artist, Re:public, situ-
ated on the corner of Republican St, is
filled with a distinctly South Lake Un-
ion type of public – ie young, tech-ish
and affluent. As a kind of microcosm
of the new neighborhood, it serves
modern farm-to-table food – artisanal
cheese plates, wild-boar Bolognese – in
a neat, minimalist space. (📞206-467-
5300; www.republicseattle.com; 429 Westlake
Ave N; mains $15-28; 🕓11am-2:30pm & 5-11pm
Mon-Thu, 10am-2am Fri & Sat, 5-11pm Sun;
🚋Westlake & Mercer)

Serious Biscuit
AMERICAN **$**

11 Map p78, F4

After **Serious Pie** (p67) comes Serious
Biscuit, Tom Douglas' first bite at the
South Lake Union cookie that has
lured so many new restaurants into
the neighborhood in the last couple of
years. The buttery biscuits (the savory
American rather than sweet British
variety) serve as flaky bases to a variety
of brunch-worthy toppings – the 'zach'
(fried chicken, gravy, bacon and egg) is
a perennial favorite. (📞206-436-0050;
www.seriouspieseattle.com/westlake; 401 West-
lake Ave N; biscuits $7-13; 🕓7am-3pm Mon-Fri,
9am-3pm Sat & Sun; 🚋Westlake & Thomas)

Dick's Drive-in
BURGERS **$**

12 Map p78, C4

If you're down to your last few dollars
and dying for something to eat, don't
panic! Dick's is calling you. Welcome to
the only fast-food joint in Seattle where
you can still buy a burger for $1.40,
along with $1.75 fries (hand cut, no
less) and $2.50 milkshakes (made with
100% ice cream, of course). (📞206-285-
5155; www.ddir.com; 500 Queen Anne Ave N;
burgers from $1.40; 🕓10:30am-2am; 🚌13)

Drinking

Hilltop Ale House
PUB

13 🍺 Map p78, B1

Hilltop is a comfy neighborhood
hangout on Queen Anne Hill, sister to
the **74th Street Ale House** (📞206-784-
2955; 7401 Greenwood Ave N; 🕓11am-11pm
Sun-Thu, 11am-midnight Fri & Sat; 🚌5) in
Green Lake. It has a friendly vibe and

✓ Top Tip

Water Activities

Lake Union is an ideal access point
for aspiring water sports enthu-
siasts. The **Northwest Outdoor
Center** (Map p78, E1; 📞206-281-9694;
www.nwoc.com; 2100 Westlake Ave N;
rental per hour from $16; 🚌62), located
on the west side of Lake Union, rents
kayaks and stand up paddle boards,
and offers tours and instruction in
sea and white-water kayaking.

a large selection of microbrews, served in proper 20oz pints, and the menu is well above your standard pub fare. (☎206-285-3877; www.seattlealehouses. com; 2129 Queen Anne Ave N; ⏰11am-11pm Sun-Thu, 11am-midnight Fri & Sat; 🚌13)

Brave Horse Tavern

PUB

14 🍺 Map p78, F5

With this place, posing as a kind of German beer hall meets Wild West saloon, Tom Douglas has made his (inevitable) lunge into the world of pubs. Brave Horse sports two dozen draft beers (local amber ales are well represented) and the place even bakes its own pretzels in a special oven. (www.bravehorsetavern.com; 310 Terry Ave N;

⏰11am-midnight Mon-Fri, 10am-midnight Sat & Sun; 🚌Terry & Thomas)

McMenamins Queen Anne

MICROBREWERY

15 🍺 Map p78, C4

The McMenamin brothers' microbrewing empire is a product of Portland, OR, but you can enjoy a comforting out-of-state taste of the brand's ever-successful blend of psychedelia meets art nouveau meets wood-paneled gentleman's club at this Lower Queen Anne perch. The real draw, of course, is the beer, including the classic Hammerhead pale ale, loaded with Oregon hops. It's kid-friendly. (www.mcmenamins. com; 200 Roy St; ⏰11am-1am; 🚼; 🚌13)

Entertainment

El Corazon
LIVE MUSIC

16 ⭐ Map p78, G5

Formerly the Off-Ramp, then Graceland, El Corazon has lots of history echoing around its walls – and lots of sweaty, beer-drenched bodies bouncing off them. Save your clean shirt for another night, and don't expect perfect sound quality at every show. The bands play loud, presumably to drown out the traffic noise from I-5 just outside the door. (📞206-381-3094; www.elcorazon seattle.com; 109 Eastlake Ave E; 🚌70)

Teatro Zinzanni
LIVE PERFORMANCE

17 ⭐ Map p78, C4

Welcome to the zany world of the 'circus dinner show,' a sort of vaudeville meets Vegas meets Cirque du Soleil. Sit back in an improvised big top for a night of jugglers, jokers, trapeze artists, music and food. The Teatro has been running since 1998 and became a permanent fixture in 2002. (www. zinzanni.com; 222 Mercer St; tickets incl dinner $99-173; 🚌13)

Shopping

REI
OUTDOOR EQUIPMENT, CLOTHING

18 Map p78, G5

As much an adventure as a shopping experience, the state-of-the-art megastore of America's largest consumer co-op has its own climbing wall – a 65ft

Brave Horse Tavern

rock pinnacle beside the store's entryway. The wall offers various options from open climbs to private instruction. Check the website for details. (📞206-323-8333; www.rei.com; 222 Yale Ave N; ⏰9am-9pm Mon-Sat, 10am-7pm Sun; 🚌70)

Queen Anne Book Company
BOOKS

19 🔒 Map p78, B2

This charming little nook is everything a neighborhood bookstore should be with frequent poetry readings and book signings. The adjoining El Diablo (p77) coffee shop has a lovely little patio where you can sip a coffee and pore over your latest book purchase. (📞206-283-5624; 1811 Queen Anne Ave N; ⏰10am-7pm Mon-Fri, 10am-5pm Sat & Sun; 🚌13)

JOHN & LISA MERRILL/GETTY IMAGES ©

Local Life
A Musical Education in Capitol Hill

Getting There

🚋 The First Hill streetcar stops at Broadway & Pine and Capitol Hill stations.

Ⓜ Capitol Hill's light rail station is on Broadway at the intersection of Denny Way.

Capitol Hill vibrates most nights to the underground sounds of Seattle. The neighborhood has witnessed quite a few musical earthquakes over the years. You won't find any stadium rockers here, but you will find small, clammy pubs and clubs providing an ideal pulpit for the best bands that no one (outside of Seattle) has ever heard of.

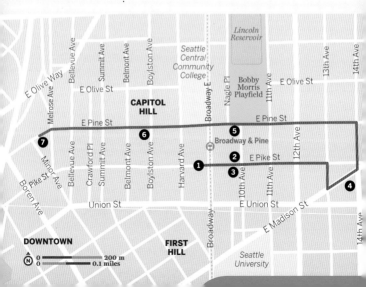

1 Pike–Pine Corridor

The Pike–Pine Corridor – a sinuous urban strip on the eastern edge of Capitol Hill – is Seattle's factory of hip: a village within a village where the city's most fashionable offspring come to party like bright young things in a plethora of unique community-run cafes, restaurants, clubs bars and shops.

2 Comet Tavern

The Comet 2.0 replaced a dirty, dive-y, grunge-era version of the **Comet** (📞206-323-9853; www.thecomettavern.com; 922 E Pike St; 🕐noon-2am; 🚊Broadway & Pine) in 2014 after a brief closure. While not as endearingly disheveled as its predecessor, the place still occupies the edgier end of the Pike–Pine ladder and now serves food (shock, horror!). Live bands sporadically rock the rafters.

3 Neumo's

Punk, hip-hop and alternative-music joint **Neumo's** (📞206-709-9442; www.neumos.com; 925 E Pike St; 🚊Broadway & Pine) is, along with the **Crocodile** (p70) in Belltown, one of Seattle's most revered small venues. Its storied list of former performers is too long to include but, if they're cool and passing through Seattle, they've probably played here.

4 Chop Suey

Chop Suey (www.chopsuey.com; 1325 E Madison St; 🕐4pm-2am Mon-Fri, 9pm-2am Sat & Sun; 🚊12) is a small dark space with high ceilings and a ramshackle faux-Chinese motif. Reborn under new ownership in 2015, it now serves burger-biased food as well as booze and music. The bookings are as mixed as the dish it's named after – electronica, hip-hop, alt-rock and other creative rumblings from Seattle's music underground.

5 Century Ballroom

For something musically different, hit the **Century Ballroom** (📞206-324-7263; www.centuryballroom.com; 915 E Pine St; 🚊Broadway & Pine) for drop-in dance lessons ($15 to $20) followed by an everyone-out-on-the-floor dance free-for-all. Styles include everything from lindy hop to salsa.

6 R Place

The Hill is Seattle's primary gayborhood and **R Place** (📞206-322-8828; www.rplaceseattle.com; 619 E Pine St; 🕐4pm-2am Mon-Fri, 2pm-2am Sat & Sun; 🚊Broadway & Pine) is one of its most flamboyant but all-round welcoming perches – a pub-club-entertainment emporium. The action is spread over three floors. Stick to the ground floor if you like it low-key. Higher-up it gets progressively saucier.

7 Baltic Room

Capitol Hill clubbers like the **Baltic Room** (📞206-625-4444; www.thebalticroom.net; 1207 Pine St; cover varies; 🕐9pm-2am; 🚊10) for its classy airs – high ceilings, wood-paneled walls, paper lanterns and an elegant balcony. As a haven of dance power, it hosts an excellent mix of local and touring DJs in a range of genres, from reggae and house to drum-and-bass.

Local Life
Parks & Pubs Around Lake Washington

The neighborhoods on Seattle's east side rarely get out-of-town visitors. If you're bored of sightseeing or were unable to uncover the soul of Seattle despite multiple visits to the Space Needle, make a trip to some of the tucked-away parks that overlook Lake Washington. A smattering of local pubs plug the gaps in between.

Getting There

🚌 Metro bus 11 runs from downtown along E Madison St all the way to Madison Park. es 2 and 3 connect downtown with Madrona via Capitol Hill.

❶ Madison Park Neighborhood

If the weather's good, Madison Park is worth visiting for its cute beach and short strip of glass-fronted cafes and restaurants. It is best reached on bus 11 along E Madison St, following an old trolley line that once bused in tired lumber workers for weekend R and R.

❷ Attic Alehouse & Eatery

Decades ago this Madison Park boozer overlooking the beach was a shooting-gallery/bowling-alley combo. The current 1960s-vintage building has morphed into the friendly **Attic Alehouse** (☎206-323-3131; 4226 E Madison St; ⏰11am-2am Mon-Fri, 8:30am-2am Sat & Sun; 🚌11) neighborhood pub, which has no inclinations to be hip. Slide in to watch the footie on the telly while enjoying a beer and a handmade burger.

❸ Denny Blaine Park

After soaking up Madison Park, head a few blocks south to lakeside **Denny Blaine Park** (200 Lake Washington Blvd E; 🚌2), which sits at the end of a looping tree-lined lane. Its more secluded location amid the luxury piles of lakeside millionaires means it sometimes attracts nude or semi-nude sunbathers.

❹ Viretta Park

Amid a lakeside nirvana of mansions lies two-tiered **Viretta Park** (🚌2), whose two graffiti-covered benches have been adopted as Seattle's unofficial Kurt Cobain memorial. The large house in which the Nirvana singer took his life in April 1994 is on the park's north side.

❺ Howell Park

Just south of Viretta Park in Madrona is a small beachfront abutting Lake Washington called **Howell Park** (🚌2). It isn't usually crowded, due to the lack of parking, and is favored by gay men in the summer. A signed trailhead leads to the beach.

❻ Madrona's 34th Ave

Madrona is a largely residential lakeside community whose adopted main street, 34th Ave, is a steep uphill climb from Madrona Park on the shores of Lake Washington. The low-key commercial strip has recently evolved to embrace a new stash of European restaurants along with a couple of good local pubs.

❼ Hi Spot Café

The **Hi Spot Café** (☎206-325-7905; www.hispotcafe.com; 1410 34th Ave; mains $10-14; ⏰7am-4pm Mon-Fri, 8am-4pm Sat & Sun; 🚌2) is a comfy little space in an old arts-and-crafts-style house in Madrona where you can get either a sit-down meal (brunch is best) or a quick espresso and pastry to go.

❽ Madrona Arms

New neighborhood pub the **Madrona Arms** (☎206-739-5104; www.madronaarms.com; 1138 34th Ave; ⏰11am-midnight Mon-Fri, 9am-2am Sat & Sun; 🚌2) is fashioned in the old British tradition with obvious nods to Seattle (local draft ales). It's run by a Northern Irishman so there's Guinness on tap and some old-country food standards, including bangers and mash.

Local Life
Cheap Thrills on 'the Ave'

The U District is like a little college town buried inside Seattle and 'the Ave,' aka University Way NW, is its heart, soul and (judging by the number of bars) liver. If you never stopped being a student, or just want to see how millennials live, plug in your culture detector at the southern end of 'the Ave' and work north.

Getting There

Ⓜ The new light-rail line links the University of Washington to Capitol Hill and downtown. The station is at the SW corner of the university campus.

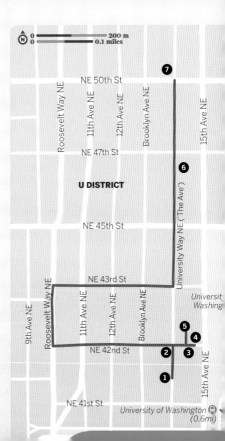

1 Big Time Microbrew & Music

Big Time (206-545-4509; www.bigtimebrewery.com; 4133 University Way NE; 11:30am-2am; 70) is one of Seattle's oldest brewpubs, conceived in 1988 – ancient history by microbrewing standards. During the school year, it can be crowded with students testing out their resistance to alcohol. For visitors, it's a good barometer of the livelier side of the University of Washington.

2 Aladdin Gyro-cery

What student nightlife strip is complete without a gyro-seller, handily poised to serve you that late-night beer soaker-upper or emergency day-after hangover 'cure'? Whether you're a student or not, the **Aladdin Gyro-cery** (206-632-5253; 4143 University Way NE; gyros $5-7.50; 10am-2:30am; 70) is an ideal place to witness the nocturnal shenanigans of 'the Ave.'

3 Orange King

Orange King (206-632-1331; 1411 NE 42nd St; burgers $3-6; 10:30am-9:30pm Mon-Fri, 3-9pm Sat; 70) is a tiny, old-fashioned greasy spoon just off 'the Ave' where you can still get an unholy mix of burgers, fries and chicken teriyaki on a starving student budget. It's not gourmet, but it's cheap and, in its own way, charming.

4 Magus Books

Seattle is an oasis of bargain bookstores, but few are as engrossing as **Magus** (206-633-1800; www.magusbooksseattle.com; 1408 NE 42nd St; 10am-8pm Sun-Thu, 10am-10pm Fri & Sat; 70). This is the kind of place where you can spend hours getting lost in crooked, narrow aisles hunting for some obscure out-of-print title that barely registers online.

5 Café Allegro

You may not know it, but the **Allegro** (206-633-3030; www.seattleallegro.com; 4214 University Way NE; drinks from $2; 6:30am-10pm Mon-Fri, 7:30am-10pm Sat, 8am-10pm Sun; 70) is a piece of history. Herein lies Seattle's oldest espresso bar, in a 1975-vintage cafe that hasn't changed much since its pioneer days. Bevies of industrious students still drop by to scribble over papers, or moon over professors, although nowadays they're frequently distracted by their cell phones.

6 Red Light

This U District thrift and vintage **shop** (206-545-4044; www.redlightvintage.com; 4560 University Way NE; 11am-8pm Mon-Sat, 11am-7pm Sun; 70) carries stylish, painstakingly selected retro clothing essential for any U-Dub hipster's wardrobe. If you want to slip into life à la mode in Seattle, it's a good place to get started.

7 U District Farmers Market

Savvy Seattleites who can't abide the crowds of Pike Place hit the U District on Saturdays for this popular but not over-crowded **market** (cnr NE 50th St & University Way NE; 9am-2pm Sat; 70). All of its displayed produce comes from an alliance of 60-plus stall-holding farmers and is grown 100% in Washington State.

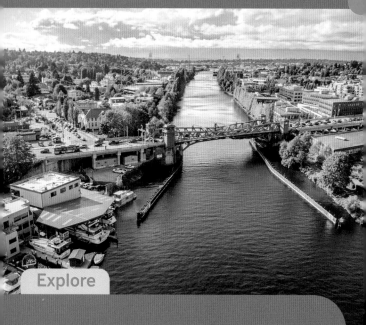

Explore

Fremont & Green Lake

Fremont pitches young hipsters among old hippies in an unlikely urban alliance, and vies with Capitol Hill as Seattle's most irreverent neighborhood, with junk shops, urban sculpture and a healthy sense of its own ludicrousness. Family-friendly Green Lake is a more affluent suburb centered on a park and favored by fitness devotees.

The Sights in a Day

☀️ Is there a better place to start a Seattle morning than electing which new coffee flavor to try at **Milstead & Co** (p99)? Only one way to find out! You may need two extra-strong shots to prepare you for the bizarre spectacle of **Fremont's Public Sculpture** (p126), which will take you the rest of the morning to decipher.

☀️ Sally north for lunch at **Paseo** (p98), a Cuban sandwich hole-in-the-wall that plenty of people travel a lot further to sample. Fortunately it's on the way to **Woodland Park Zoo** (p97), one of the US' better animal displays. Afterward, spend what's left of the afternoon watching the equally interesting Homo sapien species running, walking or rollerblading around **Green Lake Park** (p97).

🌙 Head back down to Fremont for an obligatory beer in the tasting room of **Fremont Brewing Company** (p99), followed by a farm-to-table dinner in new perch, **the Whale Wins** (p98). If you hit the right night, join the fancily attired sofa-draggers at **Fremont Almost Free Outdoor Cinema** (p98).

For a local's day in Fremont, see p94 and p126.

 Local Life

💜 **Best of Seattle**

Eating

Bars

Coffee Spots

Getting There

🚌 **Bus** Three different metro buses link Fremont to central Seattle. Bus 62 runs from downtown to Fremont and then on to Green Lake Park. Bus 5 runs from downtown via Fremont to Phinney Ridge and Woodland Park Zoo. Bus 40 originates in downtown and makes stops along Fremont's N 36th St before breezing off to Ballard.

Local Life
Fremont Taste Tour

Fremont is God's kitchen when it comes to the culinary arts. The place teems with micro-businesses all nurturing their own specialty, be it coffee, cider, beer, pies or Korean-fusion cuisine. Some of the results never leave Fremont, meaning that outsiders have all the more reason to stop by to taste the flavors and – more often than not – meet the people who produced them.

❶ Pie

It's as simple as P-I-E. Bake fresh pies daily on-site – making sure they're stuffed with homemade fillings (sweet and savory) – and serve them in a cool, bold-colored Fremont cafe. The pies at **Pie** (☎206-436-8590; www.sweet andsavorypie.com; 3515 Fremont Ave N; pies $5.95; ⏰9am-9pm Mon-Thu, to 2am Fri & Sat, 10am-6pm Sun; ☐5) are ideal for a snack lunch or you can double up and get a sweet one for dessert, too.

Broccoli-cheddar and peanut-butter-cream are crowd-pleasers.

② Fremont Coffee Company

A one-of-a-kind **coffee shop** (www.fremontcoffee.net; 459 N 36th St; ⏰6am-8pm Mon-Fri, 7am-8pm Sat & Sun; 🛜; 💻40) in an old arts-and-crafts-style house with art-adorned rooms and wicker chairs on a wraparound porch. The clientele is hip-meets-hippie, and the coffee is refreshingly strong.

③ Revel

At some point you're going to want dinner. **Revel** (📞206-547-2040; www.revelseattle.com; 403 N 36th St; small plates $12-16; ⏰11am-2pm & 5-10pm Mon-Fri, 10am-2pm & 5-10pm Sat & Sun; 💻40) is a slick, modern, Korean-American crossover restaurant (with a bit of French influence thrown in) that has quickly established itself as a big name on the Seattle eating scene thanks, in part, to its simple, shareable plates. Of note are the pork-belly pancakes and the short-rib dumplings.

④ Theo Chocolate Factory

The **Theo Chocolate Factory** (📞206-632-5100; www.theochocolate.com; 3400 Phinney Ave N; tours $10; ⏰10am-6pm, tours every half hour 10:30am-4pm; 💻40) is both a thriving local business and one of Fremont's star tourist attractions (tours are given), but if you're just passing through and want to load up with a bit of the local flavor, swing by the on-site shop to stock up on its bittersweet chocolate.

⑤ Down by the Water

If there's a flicker of sun, or temperatures start to tip 70°F, take your pie and Fremont Coffee Company java down to the water – or, more accurately, the **Fremont Cut** (the canal that connects Lake Union to the sea). Cycle paths hug both sides of a wide canal embellished by slim poplars, grassy lawns and local picnickers who sling hammocks between the trees.

⑥ Outlander Brewery & Pub

A tiny microbrewery not quite small enough to be classed as a nano-brewery, **Outlander** (📞206-486-4088; www.outlanderbrewing.com; 225 N 36th St; ⏰4-10pm Tue & Wed, 4pm-midnight Thu, 4pm-1am Fri & Sat, 2-10pm Sun; 💻40) occupies the downstairs rooms of a creaky wooden house dating from the early 1900s and provides a cozy antidote to the crowded ebullience of Fremont's other bars. It looks like someone's front room...and probably once was.

⑦ Bad Jimmy's

Follow the happy noises to this small taproom in a garage in the boxy warehouse district of West Fremont (or is it East Ballard?). Feeling more nano- than microbrewery, **Bad Jimmy's** (📞206-789-1548; www.badjimmysbrewingco.com; 4358b Leary Way NW; ⏰3pm-midnight Mon-Thu, noon-2am Fri & Sat, noon-midnight Sun; 🚹; 💻40) specializes in strongly flavored ales – be they citrus, chocolate or even coconut – with high ABVs (ie your head will be swimming after one pint).

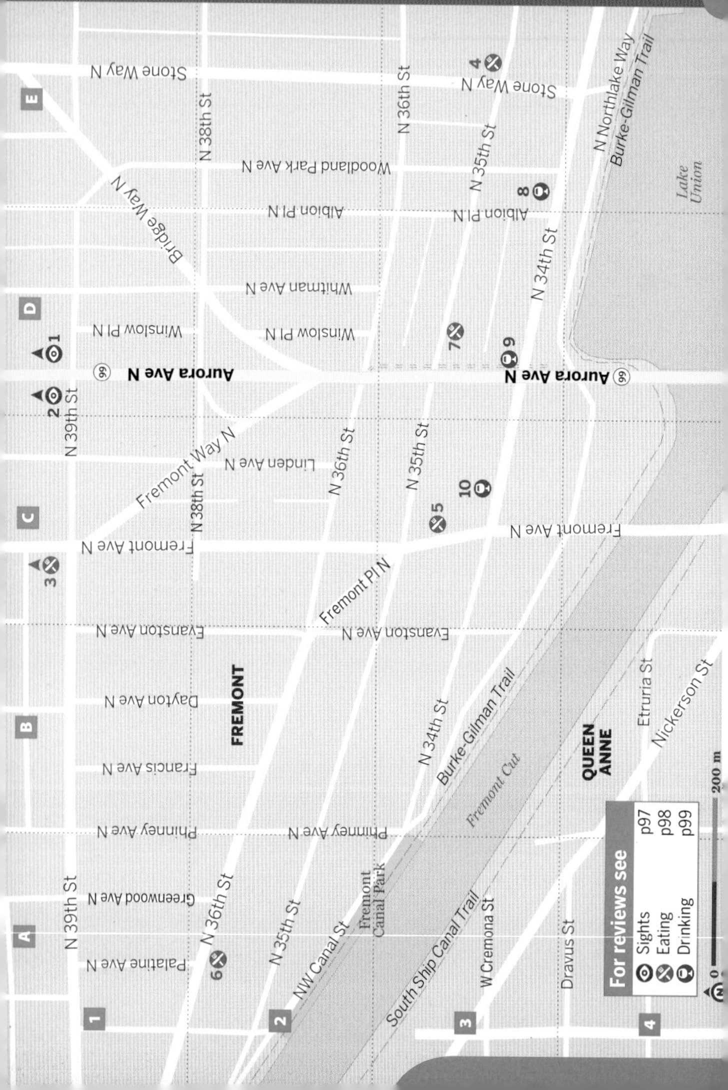

E

Stone Way N

N 38th St

N 36th St

Stone Way N

4 ✕

N Northlake Way

Burke-Gilman Trail

Woodland Park Ave N

N 35th St

N 34th St

Albion Pl N

Albion Pl N

8 ☕

Lake Union

Bridge Way N

Whitman Ave N

Winslow Pl N

Winslow Pl N

D

1 ◉

Aurora Ave N `96`

7 ✕

6 ☕

Aurora Ave N `96`

2 ◉

N 39th St

Fremont Way N

N Ave N

Linden Ave N

N 36th St

N 35th St

N 38th St

Fremont Ave N

10 ☕

5 ✕

Fremont Ave N

C

3 ✕

Fremont Ave N

Fremont Pl N

Evanston Ave N

Evanston Ave N

FREMONT

Dayton Ave N

Francis Ave N

N 34th St

Burke-Gilman Trail

Fremont Cut

QUEEN ANNE

Etruria St

Nickerson St

B

Phinney Ave N

Phinney Ave N

N 39th St

N 36th St

Greenwood Ave N

N 35th St

NW Canal St

Fremont Canal Park

Cremona St

Dravus St

A

Palatine Ave N

9 ✕

South Ship Canal Trail

W Cremona St

For reviews see	
◉ Sights	p97
✕ Eating	p98
☕ Drinking	p99

200 m

0

N

1

2

3

4

Lions at Woodland Park Zoo

Sights

Green Lake Park
PARK

1  Map p96, D1

A favorite hunting ground for runners, personal trainers and artistically tattooed sunbathers, scenic Green Lake Park surrounds a small natural lake created by a glacier during the last ice age. Two paths wind around the lake, but these aren't enough to fill the needs of the hundreds of joggers, power-walkers, cyclists and in-line skaters who throng here daily; the city government now regulates traffic on the paths. (🚍62)

Woodland Park Zoo
ZOO

2  Map p96, D1

In Woodland Park, up the hill from Green Lake Park, the Woodland Park Zoo is one of Seattle's most popular tourist attractions, consistently rated as one of the top 10 zoos in the country. It was one of the first in the nation to free animals from their restrictive cages in favor of ecosystem enclosures, where animals from similar environments share large spaces designed to replicate their natural surroundings. (☎206-548-2500; www.zoo.org; 5500 Phinney Ave N; adult/child 3-12yr May-Sep $19.95/12.25, Oct-Apr $13.75/9.25; ⏰9:30am-6pm May-Sep, 9:30am-4pm Oct-Apr; 👶; 🚍5)

Eating

Paseo   CARIBBEAN $

3 Map p96, C1

A glorified food shack whose overflowing Cuban sandwiches (which are a lot more generously stuffed than they are in Cuba) have long prompted plenty of Seattleites to re-route their daily commute in order to savor them. If you've driven this far, you shouldn't overlook the exquisitely simple rice and beans either. (☎206-545-7440; www.paseorestaurants.com; 4225 Fremont Ave N; sandwiches $8.50-11.50; ☉11am-9pm Tue-Fri, 11am-8pm Sat, 11am-6pm Sun; 🚌5)

The Whale Wins   EUROPEAN $$$

4 Map p96, E3

Forget the whale, it's the sardines that are the main winners at this eccentrically named fish-biased restaurant that shares trendy Euro-style digs with the equally hip Joule restaurant next door. The said sardines arrive on thick crispy bread spread with a heavenly mayo concoction and adorned with zesty veg. Indeed, the 'Whale' excels in veg. Have carrots and fennel ever tasted this good? (☎206-632-9425; www.thewhalewins.com; 3506 Stone Way N; mains $25-29; ☉5-10pm Mon-Sat, 5-9pm Sun; ✔; 🚌62)

Homegrown   SANDWICHES $

5 Map p96, C3

Slavishly sustainable, this locavore sandwich bar proves that green doesn't have to be tasteless. Bread is baked daily in-house and filled with unique ingredients such as split-pea pesto and pork loin rubbed in Stumptown coffee that's been laced with cayenne. Now that's what you call creative. (☎206-453-5232; www.eathomegrown.com; 3416 Fremont Ave N; half/full sandwiches $7/12; ☉8am-8pm; 🚌5)

Pomerol Restaurant   FRENCH, AMERICAN $$

6 Map p96, A2

Experienced Vietnamese-American restaurant owner serves French-influenced, contemporary American food in small but perfectly proportioned sizes in Fremont: if this concept sounds interesting, then you should probably book a table at Pomerol, one of the newer additions to Fremont's rapidly expanding restaurant universe, where seared foie gras and grilled steelhead trout share top menu credits. (☎206-632-0135; www.pomerolrestaurant.com; 127 N 36th St; mains $19-26; ⏰5-10pm Sun-Thu, 5-11pm Fri & Sat; 🚌40)

Agrodolce
ITALIAN $$$

7 Map p96, D3

Agrodolce feels more like a restaurant with a southern Italian bent than a southern Italian restaurant per se, though all the basic premises of Puglian/Sicilian cuisine are there: durum pasta, spring greens, lots of veg and, of course, fish. The spaghetti and clams merits a mention, as does the stinging-nettle pesto. The minimalist decor is warmed up by congenial neighborhood atmospherics. (☎20 6-547-9707; www.agrodolcerestaurant.net; 709 N 35th St; pasta $17-20, mains $18-30; ⏰11:30am-2:30pm & 4:30-10pm Mon-Fri, from 10am Sat & Sun; 🚌5)

Drinking

Fremont Brewing Company
BREWERY

8 Map p96, E3

This relatively new microbrewery, in keeping with current trends, sells its wares via an attached tasting room rather than a full-blown pub. Not only is the beer divine (try the seasonal bourbon barrel-aged Abominable beer), the industrial-chic tasting room and 'urban beer garden' are highly inclusive spaces, where pretty much everyone in the hood comes to hang out at communal tables. (☎20 6-420-2407; www.fremontbrewing.com; 3409 Woodland Park Ave N; ⏰11am-9pm; ⛲; 🚌62)

Milstead & Co
CAFE

9 Map p96, D3

A relatively new multi-roaster business, this fabulous neighborhood coffee bar in Fremont prefers to carefully select other people's beans rather than roast their own, but chooses them with the skill and precision of a French sommelier. The 'bean menu' changes daily, but, thanks to the expertise of owner Andrew Milstead, it rarely disappoints. (☎206-659-4814; www.milsteadandco.com; 900 N 34th St; ⏰6am-6pm Mon-Fri, 7am-6pm Sat & Sun; 📶; 🚌62)

Schilling Cider House
BAR

10 Map p96, C3

Continuing a tradition that apparently began with the Pilgrim Fathers (who allegedly smuggled a barrel of cider onto the *Mayflower*), Schilling is at the forefront of Seattle's craft cider boom, offering 32 of its fruity concoctions on draft at this woody Fremont taproom. The modus operandi: get six small taster glasses for $12 and wet your palate. (☎206-420-7088; www. schillingcider.com; 708 N 34th St; ⏰noon-11pm; 🚌62)

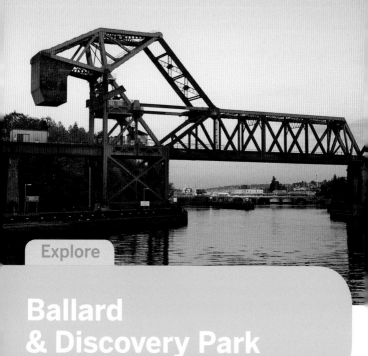

Explore

Ballard
& Discovery Park

A former seafaring community with Nordic heritage, Ballard still feels like a small town engulfed by a bigger city. Cool, independent-minded and fortified with a strong sense of its pioneer history, it's slowly being condo-ized but remains a good place to hit a brewpub or see live music. Nearby Discovery Park is a rugged pocket of coastal wilderness imported into the city.

The Sights in a Day

🔆 Get up early and shake off any Ballard beer-induced hangovers in the wonderful wild confines of **Discovery Park** (p102). A proper exploration will take all morning, but you can navigate back to Ballard by crossing the ship canal at **Hiram M Chittenden Locks** (p108), where the early 20th century engineering is exceptionally beautiful.

🔅 Skim the edge of Ballard's 'downtown' and pick up a light but flaky lunch at **Cafe Besalu** (p109). The walk north to the **Nordic Heritage Museum** (p108) is worth it. This is one of the best museums of its type in the US.

🌙 Evenings are Ballard's specialty; the neighborhood is propped up economically by its breweries these days. Start small at **Populuxe Brewing** (p110), a fledgling nano, before hitting Ballard Ave NW's aptly named **Noble Fir** (p110). Dinner temptations abound, though few leave **Bastille Cafe & Bar** (p108) without an ooh-la-la. With the night still young, follow the musical sounds and check out what alt-band is playing at the **Tractor Tavern** (p111).

For a local's day in Ballard, see p104.

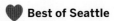

👁 Top Sights
Discovery Park (p102)

🔍 Local Life
Ballard's Bars & Beer Culture (p104)

💜 Best of Seattle

Bars
Populuxe Brewing (p110)
King's Hardware (p105)

Kids
Discovery Park (p102)
Golden Gardens Park (p108)
Card Kingdom (p111)

Eating
Cafe Besalu (p109)

Getting There

🚌 **Bus** Rapid Ride D-Line is the fastest direct bus into downtown. Metro bus 40 travels from downtown via Fremont to Ballard, stopping at multiple places in the neighborhood. For Golden Gardens Park and the Shilshole Bay Marina, you'll have to take bus 44 from the U District, or express bus 17X from downtown (weekdays only).

Top Sights
Discovery Park

A former military installation ingeniously transformed into a wild coastal park, Discovery Park is a relatively recent addition to the city landscape; it wasn't officially inaugurated until 1973. The largest green space in Seattle at 534 acres, its compact cornucopia of cliffs, meadows, dunes, forest and beaches stands as a healthy microcosm of the surrounding Pacific Northwest ecosystems and provides a welcome breathing space for hemmed in Seattleites.

👁 Map p106, A5

www.seattle.gov/parks/environment/discovery.htm

🚌33

Black-headed grosbeak at Discovery Park

Fort Lawton

The peninsula occupied by the park was originally Fort Lawton, an army base established in 1897 to protect Seattle from unnamed enemies. Fort Lawton didn't see much action until WWII, when it was used as barracks for troops bound for the Pacific theater. In the 1960s the City decided to turn it into a park, but various historic buildings from the fort remain.

Environmental Learning Center

For a map of the park's trail and road system, stop by the **Discovery Park Environmental Learning Center** (☎206-386-4236; 3801 W Government Way; ◷8:30am-5pm) near the Government Way entrance. Here you can organize educational programs, including Saturday nature walks, day camps for children and bird-watching tours.

West Point Lighthouse

The main walking trail is the 3-mile-long Loop Trail, part of a 12-mile network of marked paths. Branch off onto the South Beach trail if you want to view the still-functioning West Point Lighthouse, a great spot for panoramic views of the Sound and mountains to the west. You can circumnavigate back round to the Loop Trail via North Beach.

Daybreak Star Indian Cultural Center

Seventeen acres in the north of the park are Native American land and home to the Daybreak Star Indian Cultural Center, a community center for the United Indians of All Tribes Foundation (UIATF), a confederation of the many Native American tribes in the Seattle area. Visitor facilities are limited, but the spot offers great vistas of the Sound.

☑ Top Tips

▸ A weekend-only free shuttle runs between the Discovery Park Environmental Learning Center and South Beach (by the lighthouse) in the summer (late May to early September).

▸ There are a half dozen picnic areas in the park; the most scenic is next to the Daybreak Star Indian Cultural Center.

▸ Discovery Park has five miles of paved bike trails.

✗ Take a Break

Discovery Park is wild – there are no food concessions or cafes. However, it's a beautiful place to have a picnic. If you're coming from Ballard, stock up at Cafe Besalu (p109) or **Fresh Flours** (☎206-706-3338; www.freshflours seattle.com; 5313 Ballard Ave NW; pastries $3.50; ◷7am-5pm; ☏; ☐40). In Magnolia, the main shopping hub is on W McGraw St, between 32nd Ave W and 34th Ave W.

Local Life
Ballard's Bars & Beer Culture

Ballard's bars, breweries and pubs are befitting of a city in its own right. To eavesdrop on the neighborhood grapevine, these are the places to which you'll need to gravitate. Look out for historic, century-old bars, inventive brewpubs, gastro-pubs with carefully configured retro decor, and a nascent nano-brewing culture.

1 Frelard

You have to be an avowed Seattleite to know where 'Frelard' is, if indeed it is a neighborhood at all. The moniker is sometimes used to describe the warehouse district where western Fremont dissolves into eastern Ballard around Leary Way NW and 45th Ave. Whatever you call it, the area is replete with bars and breweries, with new places opening all the time.

❷ Jolly Roger Taproom

A secret treasure tucked away off busy Leary Way, Maritime Pacific Brewing's **Jolly Roger Taproom** (☏206-782-6181; www.maritimebrewery.com; 1111 NW Ballard Way; ⏰noon-10pm Mon-Thu, noon-11pm Fri & Sat, noon-9pm Sun; ▯Rapid Ride D-Line) is a tiny, pirate-themed bar with a nautical chart painted on the floor. These days it's less scurvy-barnacle and more placid-yachtsman, but the beer's still tops – and served in 20oz pints. Choose from 15 different microbrews.

❸ Discover Old Ballard

Ballard's historic district of old redbricked business-fronts, some with decorative embellishments, centers on Ballard Ave NW. A market sets up here on Sundays, but it's always an interesting place to stroll among legacy buildings (with plaques) letting serendipity drag you into random bars and pubs, some of which, save for a short blip during Prohibition, have been going since the early 1900s.

❹ MacLeods

Ballard's history was built on Nordic roots, but there are other 'northern' inflections to be found in **MacLeods** (☏206-687-7115; www.macleodsballard.com; 5200 Ballard Ave NW; ⏰4pm-2am; ▯40), a Scottish-style pub that sells a phone book's worth of whisky varietals in a bar overlooked by the framed countenances of notable Scots. Word on the street is that the British fish 'n' chips with mushy peas served in the adjacent eating room are the best in Ballard.

❺ King's Hardware

Ballard, like most of Seattle's neighborhoods, has changed a lot in the last couple of decades. To get a dose of some of the old-time grittiness borne out of its fishing-industry roots, decamp to **King's Hardware** (☏20 6-782-0027; www.kingsballard.com; 5225 Ballard Ave NW; ⏰3pm-2am Mon-Fri, noon-2am Sat & Sun; ▯40), where the walls are loaded with taxidermy and the scuffed wooden benches reek of marinated beer.

❻ Sexton

The **Sexton** (www.sextonballard.com; 5327 Ballard Ave NW; ⏰5-11pm Tue-Thu, 5pm-2am Fri & Sat, 10am-11pm Sun; ▯40) is unashamedly new-school Ballard, with a drinks menu that has a strong bourbon and cocktail bias (though there's still beer for the purists). The interior sports intentionally worn wood and an offbeat bar top made out of old cassettes. Creative, small-plate-style food – which you may need by this point – soaks up the booze.

❼ Ballard Beer Company

If you haven't got the time or the beer belly to tackle all of Ballard's 10+ breweries, cut to the chase at the new taproom-bottle shop at **Ballard Beer Company** (www.ballardbeercompany.com; 2050 NW Market St; ⏰noon-11pm Mon-Thu, noon-midnight Fri & Sat, noon-9pm Sun; ▯40), which offers a revolving selection of the neighborhood's best – as well as some local ciders.

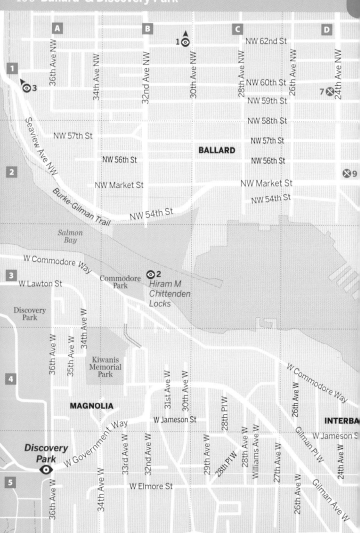

E | F | G | H

22nd Ave NW
20th Ave NW
17th Ave NW

NW 60th St
NW 59th St

BALLARD

NW 58th St
NW 57th St
NW 56th St

NW Market St
NW Market St
NW 54th St

8th Ave NW

Leary Ave NW
Ballard Ave NW
Russell Ave NW
Tallman Ave NW
Barnes Ave NW
NW Ione Pl
15th Ave NW
14th Ave NW

NW 52nd St
NW 51st St

22nd Ave NW
Shilshole Ave NW

11
4
6
12
13
14
NW Dock Pl
17th Ave NW

NW 50th St
NW 49th St

9th Ave NW

10

5

NW Leary Way

NW Ballard Way

11th Ave NW

NW Leary Way

Salmon
Bay

22nd Ave W

Elmore St

Fisherman's
Terminal

Ballard
Bridge

15th Ave NW

Fremont
Cut

0   500 m
0   0.25 miles

Sights

Nordic Heritage Museum
MUSEUM

1 Map p106, B1

Reason alone to come to Ballard – if the beer, fine food and waterside parks weren't enough – is this little gem of a museum dedicated to the brave Nordic pioneers who helped found the neighborhood (then a separate city) in the late 19th century. The museum brings together a hugely accomplished collection of stories, artifacts and other assorted treasures from Norwegian, Swedish, Finnish, Danish and Icelandic immigrants. (☏206-789-5707; www. nordicmuseum.org; 3014 NW 67th St; adult/ child $8/6; ⏱10am-4pm Tue-Sat, noon-4pm Sun; 🚌40)

Hiram M Chittenden Locks
CANAL

2 Map p106, B3

Seattle shimmers like an impressionist painting on sunny days at the Hiram M Chittenden Locks. Here, the fresh waters of Lake Washington and Lake Union drop 22ft into saltwater Puget Sound. Construction of the canal and locks began in 1911; today 100,000 boats pass through them annually. You can view fish-ladder activity through underwater glass panels, stroll through botanical gardens and visit a small museum. (3015 NW 54th St; 🚌40)

Golden Gardens Park
PARK

3 Map p106, A1

Golden Gardens Park, established in 1904 by Harry W Treat, is a lovely 95-acre beach park with sandy beaches north of Shilshole Bay Marina. There are picnic facilities, restrooms, basketball hoops, volleyball nets, gangs of Canadian geese, lots of parking and plenty of space to get away from all the activity. The Burke-Gilman Trail (p136) effectively ends here. (8498 Seaview Pl NW; 🚌45 from U District)

Eating

Bastille Cafe & Bar
FRENCH $$

4 Map p106, E3

French but not at all faux, Bastille could easily pass for a genuine Parisian bistro if it weren't for the American accents. First there's the decor: beautiful white tiles juxtaposed with black wood, mirrors and chandeliers. Then there's the menu: *moules* (mussels), *frites* (real French fries), rabbit pâté, oysters and steak (all sourced locally). (www.bastille seattle.com; 5307 Ballard Ave NW; mains $17-29; ⏱4:30pm-midnight Mon-Fri, 10am-3pm & 4:30pm-midnight Sat & Sun; 🚌40)

Walrus & the Carpenter
SEAFOOD $$

5 Map p106, F3

Puget Sound waters practically bleed oysters and – arguably – there isn't a better place to knock 'em back raw

Golden Gardens Park

with a glass of wine or two than the Walrus, a highly congenial oyster bar named not after a Beatles song but a poem by Lewis Carroll in *Through the Looking Glass*. The accolades (like the customers) keep flying in. (☎206-395-9227; www.thewalrusbar.com; 4743 Ballard Ave NW; small plates $11-14; ⏰4-10pm; 🚌40)

Stoneburner   MEDITERRANEAN $$

 6 Map p106, E3

Come and see homemade pasta prepared before your eyes in this new-ish restaurant affiliated with **Hotel Ballard** (☎206-789-5012; www.hotelballardseattle.com; 5216 Ballard Ave NW; d $329; 🛜). Pasta-rollers massage dough at workstations in full view of the diners waiting to enjoy the fruits of their labor in Stoneburner's vaguely Parisian-style bistro, a theme that doesn't look out of place here these days. (☎206-695-2051; www.stoneburnerseattle.com; 5214 Ballard Ave NW; mains $12-25; ⏰3-10pm Mon-Thu, 3-11pm Fri, 10am-11pm Sat & Sun; 🚌40)

Cafe Besalu   BAKERY, CAFE $

7 Map p106, D1

Slightly away from Ballard's 'downtown' streets, Besalu lures visitors to its isolated perch on 24th Ave with its French-style baked goods, which some bloggers have hailed as 'better than Paris.' (☎206-789-1463; www.cafebesalu.com; 5909 24th Ave NW; pastries from $2.30; ⏰7am-3pm Wed-Sun; 🚌40)

Local Life

Ballard Farmers Market

The savvy hit the **U District Farmers Market** (p91) on Saturday and breeze into **Ballard Farmers Market** (Map p106, E3; ⊙10am-3pm Sun; 🚌40) on Sunday. Do as they do and grab a cheap brunch, browse the stalls and eavesdrop about where the best bargains are to be found.

La Carta de Oaxaca   MEXICAN $$

8 Map p106, E2

One of Seattle's better Mexican places, the Oaxaca mixes hometown favorites with dishes that don't often make it north of the Rio Grande. If you've been to Guadalajara you'll know that *birria* has nothing to do with beer and plenty to do with slow-cooked lamb accompanied by roll-your-own tortillas. Order it and get your fingers dirty. (📞206-782-8722; www.lacartadeoaxaca.com; 5431 Ballard Ave NW; mains $10-25; ⊙11:30am-3pm & 5-11pm Tue-Sat, 5-11pm Mon; 🚌40)

La Isla   PUERTO RICAN $$

9 Map p106, D2

What started as a food stand at Fremont Sunday Market has become this always-packed little restaurant that offers (it claims) the only Puerto Rican cuisine in Washington. As a starter, try the *empanadillas* (little fried dough pockets filled with various savories). (📞206-789-0516; 2320 NW Market St; mains $15-21; ⊙11am-2am; 🚌40)

Drinking

Populuxe Brewing   BREWERY

10 🍺 Map p106, H3

Microbreweries too large for you? Move down a notch to a nano-brewery. The latest beer craze in Seattle favors the really little guys, such as Populuxe, who carefully nurture their beer barrel by barrel before serving it in pints and growlers from their tiny tasting room in Ballard. (📞206-706-3400; www.populuxebrewing.com; 826b NW 49th St; ⊙4:30-9pm Thu, 4:30-10pm Fri, noon-10pm Sat, 1-8pm Sun; 🚌Rapid Ride D-Line)

Noble Fir   BAR

11 🍺 Map p106, E2

Almost qualifying as a travel bookstore as well as a bar, Noble Fir's notoriously strong ales (up to 14% ABV) might fill you with enough courage to plan a hair-raising trip to the deepest Amazon (the jungle not the dot com), or somewhere equally exotic. (📞206-420-7425; www.thenoblefir.com; 5316 Ballard Ave NW; ⊙4pm-midnight Tue-Thu, 4pm-1am Fri & Sat, 1-9pm Sun; 🚌40)

Hattie's Hat   BAR

12 🍺 Map p106, E3

As long as there's a Hattie's Hat, a bit of old Ballard will always exist. This classic old divey bar has been around in some guise or other since 1904. It was last revived in 2009 but hasn't lost its charm – a perfect storm of stiff drinks, fun-loving staff and cheap, greasy-spoon food. (📞206-784-0175;

5231 Ballard Ave NW; ⊘10am-2am Mon-Fri, 9am-2am Sat & Sun; ▢40)

Entertainment

Tractor Tavern
LIVE MUSIC

13 ⭐ Map p106, E3

One of Seattle's premier venues for folk and acoustic music, the Tractor books local songwriters and regional bands, plus quality touring acts. Music runs towards country, rockabilly, folk, bluegrass and old-time. It's an intimate place with a small stage and great sound; occasional square dancing is frosting on the cake. (☏206-789-3599; www.tractortavern.com; 5213 Ballard Ave NW; ⊘8pm-2am; ▢40)

Shopping

Card Kingdom
TOYS

14 🔒 Map p106, F3

Attracting poker players, *Dungeons & Dragons* geeks, kids, board-game enthusiasts on the rebound from Vegas, Card Kingdom is the games emporium you've been dreaming about. There are plenty of organized activities here, including an on-site games parlor, but you can drop by any time it's open to browse the shelves or play a hand. (www. cardkingdom.com; 5105 Leary Ave NW; ⊘11am-midnight Mon-Fri, 10am-midnight Sat & Sun; ▢40)

Understand
Seattle's Nordic Heritage

Seattle, like many US cities, is ethnically diverse, its population concocted from a complex melange of natives and immigrants, from the original Duwamish tribe to the Hmong flower-sellers of Pike Place Market. Like the US' Upper Midwest, much of the city's early history was forged by Nordic immigrants from Norway, Sweden, Finland, Denmark and Iceland. Their arrival in such large numbers wasn't coincidental. The rain-sodden fjords, forests and mountains of Puget Sound coupled with the dominant industries of fishing and logging reminded Scandinavian settlers of home; and home it quickly became.

The bulk of Seattle's Nordic immigrants arrived in the late 19th and early 20th centuries, pushed out of their native lands by a lack of good farmland and lured to America by cheap homesteads, higher wages and religious tolerance. Nordics were instrumental in rebuilding Seattle after the 1889 Great Fire and were important in the early evolution of Ballard, then a separate city, but eerily redolent of a Norwegian fishing settlement with its burgeoning salmon industry.

You can investigate Seattle's Nordic Heritage at the eponymous museum (p108) in Ballard.

Explore

Georgetown & West Seattle

If you think that Belltown has been bleached of its bohemianism, head to Georgetown, a close-knit huddle of mildly disheveled red-brick bars and art nooks where it's still OK to be weird. On the other side of the Duwamish River, West Seattle is a detached suburban neighborhood rightly revered for its municipal beach and no-frills fish 'n' chips.

The Sights in a Day

☼ Get the water taxi to West Seattle. Strike out on foot from the dock rounding Duwamish Head to the breezy confines of **Alki Beach Park** (p117) where you can compare suntans, join a game of beach volleyball, or laugh in the face of inclement weather.

☀ Enjoy a casual fish 'n' chip lunch at **Sunfish** (p119) and take the free bus to 'the Junction' (California Ave SW and SW Alaska St) for dessert in **Bakery Nouveau** (p118) and some record-browsing in Seattle's best record store, **Easy Street** (p121). Continue by bus to the **Museum of Flight** (p114), an apt memorial to the city that spawned Boeing. You'll need two hours minimum to travel from the Wright Brothers to the jet age.

☾ Head into Georgetown proper afterwards for one of the city's most bohemian bar crawls, warming up in the positively ancient **Jules Maes Saloon** (p120). Go Mexican for dinner at **Fonda la Catrina** (p118).

◉ Top Sights
Museum of Flight (p114)

🖤 Best of Seattle
Eating
Bakery Nouveau (p118)

Activities
Alki Beach Park (p117)

Flip Flip Ding Ding (p120)

Bars
Machine House Brewery (p120)

Getting There

🚌 **Bus** Metro buses 106 and 124 run frequently from downtown to Georgetown. Bus 124 carries on to the Museum of Flight (p114). Rapid Ride C-Line runs from downtown to West Seattle.

⚓ **Boat** Hourly water taxis leave Pier 50 from the downtown waterfront to Seacrest Park in West Seattle. There's no weekend service in the winter.

Top Sights
Museum of Flight

The city that spawned Boeing, not surprisingly, coughs up one of the nation's finest aviation museums, chronicling flight history from Kitty Hawk to Concorde. It's a multifarious affair gluing together a broad sweep of flying-related memorabilia in several hangar-sized galleries. The exhibits include some of the most ingenious human-made objects that have defied gravity: picture nefarious V2 rockets, Apollo lunar modules and aerodynamic gliders.

Map p116, C5

206-764-5720

www.museumofflight.org

9404 E Marginal Way S, Boeing Field

adult/child $21/13, 5-9pm 1st Thu of month free

9am-5pm

124

Great Gallery

The centerpiece of the museum is a humongous gallery filled with historic aircraft that overhang chronological exhibits on the history of flight. If you're short on time, jump-cut to the **Tower**, a mock-up of an air traffic control tower overlooking the still operational Boeing Field. Another must-see is a replica of the Wright Brothers' original 1903 *Wright Flyer*.

Red Barn

Saved in the 1970s when it was floated upriver from its original location 3km away, this two-story red barn dating from 1909 was Boeing's original manufacturing space. It is filled with the early history of flight, with a strong bias toward the Boeing business.

J Elroy McCaw Gallery

In the separate J Elroy McCaw Gallery, sandwiched between the Red Barn and museum cafe, is a hugely impressive collection of WWI and WWII warplanes from rickety looking biplanes to a Lockheed Lightning long-range fighter. Caption boards relate tumultuous tales of the Red Baron and Spitfire scrambles.

Aviation Pavilion

The new Aviation Pavilion opened in 2016 and is accessible via a modernist bridge over E Marginal Way. It displays a half dozen iconic planes that you can look inside, including a British Airways **Concorde**; the first jet-powered **Air Force One**, used by presidents Eisenhower, Kennedy, Johnson and Nixon; and a **Boeing 727** prototype.

☑ Top Tips

▶ Entry is free the first Thursday of each month from 5pm to 9pm.

▶ Ask at reception about the free tours with an aviation expert that run several times daily.

▶ For an extra $2 you can watch a flying-themed film in 3D at the on-site theater.

▶ Also available are behind-the-scenes tours of the adjacent Boeing Field (Seattle's original airport). They run at 11:30am and 1:30pm on weekends from May to October and cost $20.

✗ Take a Break

Since it's situated 2.5 miles from the nearest eating strip in George-town, your best bet for refreshment at the museum is in the on-site **Wings Cafe**, where you can enjoy chunky sandwiches, salads, coffee and muffins, overlooking the Boeing Field runways.

SODO

S Dawson St

S Bennett St S

S Brandon St

S Lucile St

S Findlay St

S Orcas St

S Homer St

S Mead St

S Orcas St

S Fidalgo St

GEORGETOWN

S Front St

S Michigan St

S River St

E Marginal Way S

S Warsaw St

S Eddy St

S Bailey St

S Albro Pl

S Hardy St

4th Ave S

5th Ave S

6th Ave S

7th Ave S

5th Pl S

Denver Ave S

5th Ave S

6th Ave S

Airport Way S

Corson Ave S

Carleton Ave S

Flora Ave S

Ellis Ave S

Stanley Ave S

Airport Way S

13th Ave S

15th Ave

BEACON HILL

S Dawson St

S Bennett St S

S Lucile St

15th Ave S

Georgetown Playfield

Corson Ave S

S Homer St

S Doris St

S Nebraska La

S Vale St

S Harney St

Airport Way S

S Willow St

E Marginal Way S

S Myrtle St

Museum of Flight

Boeing Field/ King County International Airport

For reviews see	
 Top Sights	p114
Sights	p117
Eating	p118
Drinking	p119
Shopping	p121

400 m
0.2 miles

Alki Beach Park

Sights

Alki Beach Park
BEACH, PARK

1 ◉ Map p116, C1

Alki Beach has an entirely different feel from the rest of Seattle: this 2-mile stretch of sand could almost fool you into thinking it's California, at least on a sunny day, except for the obvious lack of...Californians. There's a bike path, volleyball courts on the sand, and rings for beach fires. (🚌775 from Seacrest Dock)

Duwamish Head
LANDMARK

2 ◉ Map p116, C1

Popular for its views of Elliott Bay and downtown, this relatively tranquil spot was once painted with a different hue. In 1907 a huge amusement park, Luna Park, opened here. In its days as a loud and over-the-top attraction, the park covered more than 10 acres and hosted the 'longest bar on the bay.' This grand assertion unfortunately led to claims of debauchery and carousing, and the park was eventually closed in 1913 by the conservative powers-that-were. (🚌775 from Seacrest Dock)

Krab Jab Studio
GALLERY

3 ◉ Map p116, C2

You never know what you're going to get at this small gallery inside the old redbrick Rainier beer factory

Top Tip

Art Attack

Georgetown's industrial art scene pulls together on the second weekend of each month at the **Georgetown Second Saturday Art Attack**. This is the best time to visit the neighborhood's myriad galleries, some of which have rather sporadic opening hours. Almost the entire commercial strip takes part in the monthly event, which runs from 6pm to 9pm and exhibits work in cafes, pubs, galleries and studios. Complimentary drinks and snacks are often laid on.

in Georgetown, which leans heavily toward 'fantasy art.' At last visit they were displaying a sculpture called *I am the Walrus* depicting scenes from the Beatles song. Krab Jab opens extended hours during Georgetown's 'Art Attack' (6pm to 9pm second Saturday of the month). (www.krabjab studio.com; 5628 Airport Way S; ⏱1-6pm Fri & Sat)

Eating

Bakery Nouveau BAKERY $

5 Map p116, C1

No discussion of Seattle's best bakery omits Bakery Nouveau. The crumbly, craggy almond and chocolate croissants are as addictive as other substances far worse for your health. (www.bakerynou veau.com; 4737 California Ave SW; baked goods

from $1.50; ⏱6am-7pm Mon-Fri, 7am-7pm Sat & Sun; ☐Rapid Ride C-Line)

Fonda la Catrina MEXICAN $$

5 Map p116, C2

The search to find a decent Mexican restaurant in Seattle comes to an end in Georgetown in the busy confines of Fonda la Catrina, where Day of the Dead iconography shares digs with Diego Rivera-like murals and – more importantly – fabulous food. Offering way beyond the standard taco-burrito-enchilada trilogy, this place puts soul into its Latino cooking. (⏰206-767-2787; www.fondalacatrina.com; 5905 Airport Way S; tacos & tamales $9; ⏱11am-11pm Mon-Fri, 10am-midnight Sat, 10am-10pm Sun; ☐124)

Brass Tacks AMERICAN $$

6 Map p116, D3

Of all the redbrick drinking houses that line Georgetown's Airport Way S, Brass Tacks is the most 'gourmet' place. Here you can sit at the bar and imbibe your beer with creative meat dishes while listening to the resident jazz trio. The standout dish? Not meat, but the brussels sprouts fried with blue cheese, lemon aioli and garlic. (⏰206-397-3821; www.georgetownbrass.com; 6031 Airport Way S; mains $14-25; ⏱11am-10pm Tue & Wed, 11am-11pm Thu-Sat, 10am-3pm Sun; ☐124)

Salty's on Alki STEAK, SEAFOOD $$$

7 Map p116, C1

Salty's isn't actually on Alki Beach; rather it's on the other side of

Duwamish Head facing Elliott Bay. In any case, the view of the Seattle skyline combined with the deluxe steak-and-seafood menu make this a big enough lure for people all over Seattle. Eschewing the fish 'n' chips frugality of the rest of West Seattle, this place is distinctly upmarket. (☑206-937-1600; www.saltys.com; 1936 Harbor Ave SW; mains $26-46; ☺11am-9pm Mon-Fri, 8:45am-9pm Sat, 9:30am-9pm Sun; 🌿Seacrest Dock)

Marination Ma Kai

HAWAIIAN, KOREAN $

8 Map p116, C1

What do you get when you cross Hawaiian cuisine with the food of Korea? A Pacific marriage made in heaven if the fish tacos and kimchi quesadillas at Marination Ma Kai are anything to go by. (☑206-328-8226; www.marinationmobile.com; 1660 Harbor Ave SW; snacks $3-12; ☺11am-8pm Mon-Thu, 9am-9pm Fri & Sat, 9am-8pm Sun; 🌿Seacrest Dock)

Via Tribunali

PIZZA $$

9 Map p116, C3

This small Seattle-founded chain operates in four of the city's hipper sanctums (including Capitol Hill and Fremont) plus a couple of foreign enclaves (NYC and Portland, OR). It deals not in pizzas but *pizze*: crisp-crusted Italian pies that are true to the food's Neapolitan roots. (☑206-464-2880; www.viatribunali.net; 6009 12th Ave S; pizze $15-19; ☺11am-11pm Mon-Thu, 11am-midnight Fri, 4pm-midnight Sat, 3-10pm Sun; 🚌124)

Local Life
West Seattle Fish 'n' Chips

You haven't really been to Alki until you've tried the fish 'n' chips. For locals, there are two institutions: **Spud Fish & Chips** (☑206-938-0606; www.alkispud.com; 2666 Alki Ave SW; fish & chips $6-16; ☺11am-9pm; 🚌775 from Seacrest Dock) and **Sunfish** (☑206-938-4112; 2800 Alki Ave SW; fish & chips $6-11; ☺11am-9pm Tue-Sun; 🚻; 🚌775 from Seacrest Dock), where deep-fried greatness is achieved with lashings of cod, halibut, salmon, fried oysters, clam strips and, of course, thick-cut chips. Sit at an outdoor table overlooking the beach and enjoy the boardwalk feel.

Drinking

Conservatory

CAFE

10 Map p116, C2

Hit this bohemian cafe on the right night and you'll feel as if you've slipped into a Freudian dream and woken up in 19th-century Vienna. The Conservatory, with its random art easels, mini-skeletons and piles of dusty books, models itself on the European coffee shops of the 1800s. Far more than just a cafe, it hosts regular figure-drawing sessions and other esoteric art happenings. (☑206-420-3037; www.theconservatoryseattle.com; 5813 Airport Way S; ☺8am-6pm; 🛜; 🚌124)

Machine House Brewery

MICROBREWERY

11 Map p116, C2

If you want to enjoy a beer in Georgetown's erstwhile redbrick Rainier beer factory, head to this minimalist tap room and microbrewery where old-fashioned hand pumps dispense classic British-style ales that are big on taste but not too high in alcohol per volume. Bonus: it's kid-friendly and shows British soccer games on the big screen. (206-432-6025; www.machinehousebrewery.com; 5840 Airport Way S; 3-9pm Wed-Fri, noon-9pm Sat, noon-6pm Sun; 124)

Jules Maes Saloon

BAR

12 Map p116, C2

You can pretty much imbibe the beer off the wallpaper in Seattle's oldest surviving pub: it's been offering liquor since 1888, when the city

Local Life
Flip Flip Ding Ding

Pinball is currently undergoing a renaissance in Seattle (computer games be damned!) and its popularity is exemplified in places such as **Flip Flip Ding Ding** (Map p116, C3; 206-508-0296; 6012 12th Ave S; noon-midnight Mon-Fri, 4pm-midnight Sat & Sun; 124), a wonderfully named bar–pinball emporium, which opened in 2014. Boisterous tournaments kick off most weekends.

was a youthful 37 years old. Once a speakeasy and allegedly haunted, it still manages a shaky juxtaposition of traditional saloon (pinball and other vintage games) and modern bar (punk rock and tattoos). (20 6-957-7766; 5919 Airport Way S; 10am-2am; 124)

Elliott Bay Brewery & Pub

BREWERY

13 Map p116, C1

Long and narrow, with a loft at the back of the room and a beer garden outdoors, this comfortable brewpub makes a nice retreat after a day at Alki Beach. All the beers are organic and range from the light Luna Weizen to the heavy-hitting Demolition IPA. (206-932-8695; www.elliottbaybrewing.com; 4720 California Ave SW; 11am-midnight Mon-Sat, 11am-11pm Sun; Rapid Ride C-Line)

Smarty Pants

BAR

14 Map p116, D3

This redbrick industrial hangout for scooterists and sport-bike riders has a number of vintage motorcycles propped up in the windows, a hearty sandwich menu ($7 to $9; plus a weekend brunch) and an obvious fondness for two-wheeled mischief of all types. Wednesday is Bike Night, when fans watch the week's recorded races. (206-762-4777; www.smartypantsseattle.com; 6017 Airport Way S; 11am-midnight Mon-Fri, 9am-midnight Sat, 9am-4pm Sun; 124)

Easy Street Records & Café

Shopping

Easy Street Records & Café

MUSIC

15 🔒 Map p116, D1

Pearl Jam once played at Easy Street, arguably Seattle's most multifarious record store, and the business continues to sponsor regular events. Inside, young kids with elaborate tattoos mingle with graying ex-punks under a montage of retro parking signs and old Nirvana posters. Proving itself to be an invaluable community resource, Easy Street has its own on-site cafe selling food, coffee and beer. (📞206-938-3279; www.easystreetonline.com; 4559 California Ave SW; ⏱9am-9pm; 🚌Rapid Ride C-Line)

Fantagraphics Bookstore & Gallery

BOOKS

16 🔒 Map p116, C3

Founded in the 1970s on the East Coast, this cool alt-comic and graphic-book publisher moved to Seattle in the late '80s and opened this one-of-a-kind bookstore-gallery in 2006. Stocked with quirky books, comics and magazines, and furnished in an exhibition space that hosts monthly shows and readings, it's well worth making a pilgrimage out to Georgetown for. (📞206-658-0110; www.fantagraphics.com; 1201 S Vale St; ⏱11:30am-8pm Mon-Sat, 11:30am-5pm Sun; 🚌124)

The Best of
Seattle

Seattle's Best Walks

Seattle's Best...

View of Seattle from Kerry Park
TOTORORO/GETTY IMAGES ©

Best Walks
Downtown Architecture

🏃 The Walk

Downtown Seattle isn't the city's most buzzing or creative neighborhood, but its tall, modern skyscrapers contain some interesting architectural details rarely spared a glance by the suited office workers who hurry from building to building at street level. This walk incorporates the most important examples of Seattle's skyscraper 'art' from early art deco to 21st century ultra-modernism.

Start Arctic Building; 🚊 Pioneer Square

Finish Westlake Center; 🚊 Westalke

Length 1 mile; 45 minutes

✕ Take a Break

You're so close to Pike Place Market that it would be foolish not to dive into its welcoming melee to satisfy your cravings. Countless cheap eats make tempting entreaties. **Beecher's Handmade Cheese** (p33) is a perennial favorite.

Arctic Building

❶ Arctic Building

The Arctic building was constructed in 1917 as an eponymous club started by Klondike gold-rush veterans. Its defining feature is the 25 walrus heads that embellish the building's exterior a couple of floors up. After admiring their tusks, walk up Cherry St and take a left onto 4th Ave.

❷ Columbia Center

Taking up the block between 4th and 5th Aves and Columbia and Cherry Sts, the Columbia Center (p32) is the tallest building on the West Coast. If you have time (and $14), check out the observation deck on the 73rd floor.

❸ Safeco Plaza

Built in 1969, the Safeco Plaza was one of Seattle's first real skyscrapers, ending the Space Needle's short seven-year reign at the top. The building ushered in an era of massive downtown growth – most of it in a vertical direction. It is now Seattle's fifth-tallest building.

4 Seattle Central Library

Spectacular from the outside with its rough-cut diamond shape, Seattle's glass-heavy library (p32) is worth a peek inside. Go for a quick ride up its lime-green escalators to see how good architecture can combine practicality and beauty. There are wide-ranging views from the top levels.

5 1201 Third Avenue

The magnificence of the Seattle skyline is reflected in the 55-story 1201 Third Avenue building at 3rd Ave and Seneca, which changes colors with the clouds and sunsets. This is the second-tallest building in Seattle and dates from 1988. Seattleites have nicknamed it 'the Spark Plug.'

6 Rainier Tower

With its inverted base looking like a tree that's been nibbled by a beaver, Rainier Tower has been nicknamed the 'beaver building.' Taking up an entire block between 4th and 5th Aves and University and Union Sts is Rainier Square, a shopping center connected to the top-heavy tower.

7 Fairmont Olympic Hotel

The Jazz Age Fairmont Olympic Hotel dates from 1924 and is undoubtedly one of the classiest remnants of Seattle's early-20th-century heyday. The block-square building looks sober and unrevealing on the outside, but journey through the revolving doors to discover a plush lobby.

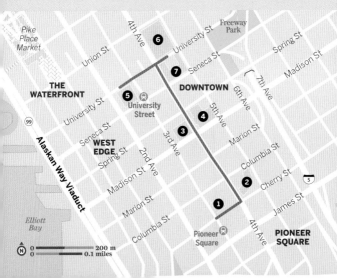

Best Walks
Center of the Universe

🏃 The Walk

A tongue-in-cheek guidepost located in the middle of Fremont claims to mark the 'Center of the Universe.' It's just one of numerous outlandish statues and sculptures that decorate several square blocks on the southern edge of the neighborhood abutting the Washington Ship Canal (also known as the Fremont Cut). While not providing any concrete evidence of Fremont's intergalactic situation, this walk offers a short but suitably surreal stroll past its best pieces of outdoor art.

Start Fremont Rocket; 🚌 40

Finish Apatosaurs; 🚌 40

Length 0.75 miles; one hour

✕ Take a Break

Fremont Brewing Company (p99)

Fremont Troll, by artists Steve Badanes, Will Martin, Donna Walter and Ross Whitehead

WOLFGANG KAEHLER/GETTY IMAGES ©

❶ Fremont Rocket

Start this unusual walk on Evanston Ave N between N 35th and N 36th Sts at the rather conspicuous Fremont Rocket, Fremont's community totem, a real-life Cold War rocket that never took off. Salvaged from a Belltown army surplus store in 1993, it's now grafted surreally onto the corner of a shoe shop.

❷ Lenin Statue

Head north up Evanston Ave N to N 36th St. On N 36th St at Fremont Place N, you'll see a controversial addition to Fremont's collection of public art: a bronze, 16ft statue of former communist leader Vladimir Lenin weighing seven tons. Brought to the USA from Czechoslovakia in 1993, it's technically for sale.

❸ Fremont Troll

Continue east along Fremont Place N, cross Fremont Ave N and go east on N 35th St. When you reach the dark, shadowy space where the Aurora Bridge meets the ground look to the left. Here lurks the *Fremont Troll*, an 18ft cement figure busily munching on a VW Beetle, an oblique reference to the children's story *The Three Billy Goats Gruff*.

❹ Late for the Interurban

Head south down Troll Ave underneath the concrete supports of the Aurora Bridge, which resemble the nave of a giant Gothic church. Turn right on N 34th St toward Fremont Bridge. Here you'll pass a life-size statue of two clowns pulling in opposite directions known as *Late for the Interurban*.

❺ Waiting for the Interurban

A couple of minutes later you'll fall upon what they're late for: namely Seattle's most popular piece of public art, *Waiting for the Interurban*, depicting a group of hapless commuters waiting for a train that never comes. The statue is regularly 'dressed up' by artistic locals as a show of creativity, protest or good old humor.

❻ Apatosaurs

Go west past Fremont Bridge and along N 34th St for two blocks to Phinney Ave N. Along the banks of the ship canal and abutting the Burke-Gilman Trail, you'll see two life-size apatosauruses fashioned out of ivy that were given to Fremont by the Pacific Science Center in 1999. The adult dinosaur measures 66ft-long, making it the world's largest known topiary.

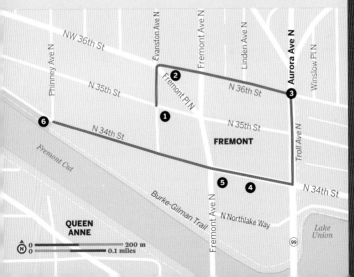

Best
Restaurants

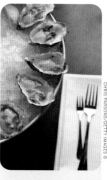

CHRIS PARSONS/GETTY IMAGES ©

If you want to get a real taste for eating in Seattle, dip your metaphorical finger into Pike Place Market. This clamorous confederation of farmers, artisan bakers, cheese producers, fishers and family-run fruit stalls is the gastronomic bonanza that every locavore dreams about, and its cheap, sustainable, locally produced food ends up at just about every Seattle restaurant that matters.

What is Northwest Cuisine?

A lot of Seattle's gourmet restaurants describe their food as 'Northwest cuisine.' Its cornerstone is high-quality regional ingredients that grow abundantly in Washington State: seafood so fresh it squirms, fat berries freshly plucked, mushrooms dug out of the rich soil and a cornucopia of fruit and vegetables. Another distinguishing feature is pan-Asian cooking, often referred to as Pacific Rim cuisine or fusion food. The blending of American or European standards with ingredients from Asia results in some unusual combinations – don't be surprised if you get wasabi on your French fries.

Mold-breaking Chefs

Tom Douglas The biggest name on the Seattle food scene, Douglas helped define what people mean when they talk about Northwest cuisine. He opened his first restaurant, Dahlia, in 1989 and has followed it with 16 more. Douglas won the prestigious James Beard Award for Best Restaurateur in 2012 and once battled Masaharu Morimoto in an episode of *Iron Chef America* – and won.

Ethan Stowell With 12 Seattle restaurants, Stowell is now considered an established star. His specialty is marrying creative Italian cuisine with classic Northwest ingredients, especially seafood.

☑ **Top Tip**

▶ Surrounded by water, Seattle is an obvious powerhouse of fresh seafood. Seek out the local favorites including Dungeness crab, salmon, halibut, oysters, spot prawns and clams.

Asian Restaurants

Wild Ginger All kinds of Asian cuisine under the same downtown roof. (p34)

Tamarind Tree Hidden-away Vietnamese spot in Little Saigon that's become something of a city legend. (p49)

Shiro's Sushi Restaurant Japanese food as art in the heart of Belltown. (p67)

Jade Garden The best in dim sum in the International District. (p50)

Budget

Crumpet Shop Pike Place phenomenon where thick toppings are lashed on homemade crumpets. (p34)

Piroshky Piroshky Russian buns are rolled in the window of this Pike Place Market hole-in-the-wall. (p33)

Top Pot Hand-Forged Doughnuts The champagne of doughnuts. (p66)

Bakery Nouveau Best bakery this side of...Paris. (p118)

Italian Restaurants

Pink Door Ristorante Where else can you eat *linguine alle vongole* with a trapeze artist flying over your head? (p34)

Tavolàta Northwest meets Italian cuisine over an open kitchen in Belltown. (p66)

Serious Pie Seriously good pizzas with novel toppings. (p67)

Bakeries

Bakery Nouveau Destination bakery that's worth crossing town to West Seattle for – now in Capitol Hill too! (p118)

Piroshky Piroshky Insanely popular Russian bakery with perennial queues. (p33)

Macrina Watch bread dough being kneaded through a shop window in Belltown. (p66)

Cafe Besalu Locally tipped French-style bakery in an out-of-the-way nook in Ballard. (p109)

Sandwiches

Paseo Generously stuffed Cuban sandwiches in Fremont that require *muchos* napkins. (p98)

Homegrown Sustainable and eco-conscious purveyor of fine sandwiches. (p98)

Macrina Bakery with affiliated cafe where you can order your sandwiches made with bread fresh from the oven. (p66)

Worth a Trip

The king of all locavore restaurants, **Sitka & Spruce** (☎206-324-0662; www.sitkaandspruce.com; 1531 Melrose Ave; plates $12-33; ⏱11:30am-2pm & 5-10pm Mon-Fri, 10am-2pm & 5-11pm Sat, 10am-2pm & 5-9pm Sun; ✦; ☐10) was the pilot project of celebrated Seattle chef Matt Dillon. It's since become something of an institution and a trend-setter with its small-country-kitchen decor and constantly changing menu concocted with ingredients from Dillon's own farm. Sample items include the house-made charcuterie or roasted asparagus and liver parfait.

Best
Coffee Spots

When the first Starbucks opened in Pike Place Market in 1971, Seattle was suddenly the center of the coffee universe. It still is, although these days Starbucks is rivaled by numerous 'third wave' coffee shops that buy fair-trade coffee with traceable origins and roast it in-house through a micro-managed process that pays attention to everything from bean quality to 'taste notes.'

Local Coffee Chainlets

Unless you fell asleep in 1984 and have just woken up, the word 'Starbucks' needs no elaboration. But Seattle hosts a number of other smaller coffee 'chainlets,' many of which only have branches in the city and its suburbs.

Uptown Espresso Founded in Lower Queen Anne in the mid-1980s, it now has eight locations and is known for its 'velvet foam' and generous opening hours.

Caffe Ladro Another Queen Anne–founded cafe, Ladro now has 15 branches. It roasts its own beans and bakes its own snacks daily.

Zoka Coffee Four cafes. The huge U District cafe is typical of the brand and perennially full of students.

Storyville Coffee Company One of Seattle's newer cafes, Storyville is definitively upmarket with a slick strip-wood counter and a veritable army of staff who'll take their time to pull you the finest cuppa.

Caffe Vita Founded in Queen Anne in the mid-90s, Vita has cast its net way beyond Seattle to open cafes in LA, New York and Portland.

Victrola Coffee Roasters Unashamedly retro Victrola puts quality over quantity in its cafes. Expect knowledgeable baristas, home-roasted beans and free public cuppings every Wednesday.

☑ **Top Tip**

▶ Road Dogs is known for its brewery tours, but it also offers two daily two-hour Seattle coffee tours stopping off at cafes and microroasters. See www.roaddogtours.com for bookings and details.

One-of-a-kind coffee shops

Zeitgeist Coffee At Zeitgeist it's all about the coffee – and the gorgeous almond croissants. (p50)

Milstead & Co Multiroaster in Fremont choosing the best coffee on the market; menu changes daily. (p99)

El Diablo Coffee Co Cuban-style coffee served with Cuban-style

Starbucks Reserve Roastery & Tasting Room

snacks in the salubrious confines of Queen Anne. (p77)

Italian Coffee

Caffè Umbria Small chain that roasts its own beans; main cafe in Pioneer Square. (p51)

Caffè Torino True to its Turin roots, this place serves Lavazza coffee and *bicerins* (Italian chocolate-coffee mix). (p82)

Places for coffee and a snack

Top Pot Hand-Forged Doughnuts The doughnuts are the stars here, although the coffee's not far behind. (p66)

Zeitgeist Coffee Cafe whose almond croissants

go down nicely with an 8oz latte. (p50)

Caffe Ladro Pastries baked fresh every day at the special Ladro bakery. (p82)

Neighborhood Cafes

Caffè Fiore Local favorite tucked away in a salubrious side-street in Queen Anne. (p77)

El Diablo Coffee Co Locals atop Queen Anne hill love their Cuban-style coffee. (p77)

Fremont Coffee Company Heritage house turned cozy coffee shop in Fremont. (p95)

Café Allegro Hive of busy undergraduate life in the U District. (p91)

Worth a Trip

This new-ish and so far unique **Starbucks Reserve Roastery & Tasting Room** (www.starbucks.com/roastery; 1124 Pike St; coffees $3-12; ⊘7am-11pm) in Capitol Hill is the antithesis of everything Starbucks-y that has gone before. Even Starbucks-phobes will find something to like here, be it the tasting menu, the coffee library, the huge copper casks, the micro- and small-batch roasters or the custom-made retro furniture.

Best
Bars

It's hard to complain too much about Seattle's weather when the two best forms of rainy-day solace – coffee and beer – are available in such abundance. No doubt about it, Seattle's an inviting place to enjoy a drink, whatever your poison. Adding fresh flavors to an already complex brew is an obsession with microdistilleries and cider houses.

Macro Amounts of Microbrews

The microbrew explosion rocked the Northwest around the same time as the gourmet-coffee craze, and not coincidentally: Seattle's Redhook Brewery was cofounded in 1981 by Gordon Bowker, one of the guys who founded Starbucks.

Most local microbreweries started out as tiny craft breweries that produced European-style ales. Many of these small producers initially lacked the capital to offer their brews for sale anywhere but in the brewery building itself, hence the term brewpub – an informal pub with its own on-site brewery.

Though you can find microbrews at almost every bar in town, brewpubs often feature signature beers and ales not available anywhere else. It's worth asking about specialty brews or seasonal beers on tap.

Microdistilleries

Not content with helping to shape North America's microbrewing revolution in the 1980s and '90s, Seattle has recently embraced further alcohol-inspired craftsmanship in the shape of microdistilled spirits. Though the trend is evident all over the US, Washington State is – as ever – at the vanguard, harboring a fifth of the nation's microdistilleries, all of them churning out meticulously produced small-batch tipples of gin, vodka, whiskey, brandy and even limoncello.

☑ **Top Tips**

▶ If you're a beer aficionado, hit the neighborhood of Ballard, which has by far the best selection of pubs, bars and microbreweries.

▶ Other good places to go on a bar crawl are 2nd Ave in Belltown and the Pike–Pine Corridor in Capitol Hill.

Brewpubs & Tasting Rooms

Fremont Brewing Company New cavernous brewery where you can taste beer at wooden tables on the factory floor. (p126)

Populuxe Brewing New Ballard nano-brewery with the atmosphere of a well-worn village pub. (p110)

Pike Pub & Brewery One of the oldest and most cherished brewpubs in Seattle. (p35)

Machine House Brewery Small, friendly peddler of British-style ales in an old Georgetown beer factory. (p120)

Good Old-Fashioned Pubs

Owl & Thistle Genuine Irish pub with good music and cheap fish 'n' chips in downtown. (p37)

Madrona Arms New pub with a lived-in feel plying British-style beer in Madrona. (p89)

Specialist Bars

Zig Zag Café Long-standing shaker and stirrer of Seattle's finest cocktails. (p36)

Schilling Cider House Fremont tasting room that's at the forefront of Seattle's latest hard cider craze. (p99)

Bookstore Bar Comfy hotel bar specializing in bourbon and whiskey. (p36)

The Whisky Bar Freshly relocated Belltown haven of the 'water of life.' (p70)

Dives

Shorty's Punk rock, hard liquor and pinball – a lethal combination. (p70)

Five Point Café Proudly disheveled relic of pre-hipster Belltown. (p70)

Comet Tavern What the word 'grunge' was invented for. (p87)

King's Hardware Ballard's old-school rendezvous of bikers and tattoos. (p105)

Worth a Trip

On a drizzly day in Puget Sound, the damp essence of Seattle isn't a million miles from the Western Isles of Scotland, a comparison not lost on the precocious young whiskey-makers of **Westland** (206-767-7250; www.westlanddistillery.com; 2931 1st Ave S; 11am-6pm Tue-Thu, 11am-8pm Fri & Sat; SoDo). Visit their SoDo headquarters for an informal but informative distillery tour followed by a throat-warming tipple of the 'water of life.'

Best
Live Music

MAT HAYWARD/SHUTTERSTOCK ©

Quietly aggrieved that it was being bypassed by big-name touring acts in the 1980s, Seattle shut itself away and created its own live-music scene. This explosive grassroots movement is backed up by plenty of other artistic strands, including independent cinema, burlesque theater, bookshop poetry readings and some high-profile opera, classical music and drama.

Alt-Rock Venues

Crocodile Nationally renowned midsize live venue that helped promote grunge. (p70)

Neumo's The other pillar of Seattle's dynamic scene has been updated and remains relevant. (p87)

Chop Suey Diverse selection of live acts, with indie alternating with hip-hop. (p87)

Tractor Tavern The anchor of Ballard's live scene specializes in alt country. (p111)

Jazz

Dimitriou's Jazz Alley Sophisticated jazz club in Belltown that bags the best touring acts. (p70)

Triple Door Jazz is just one of the myriad musical forms that enlighten this plush dinner club. (p37)

Tula's Jazz Intimate venue for mainly local acts on Belltown's nightlife strip. (p63)

Classical

Seattle Symphony One of the US' finest orchestras plays in Seattle's finest concert hall, Benaroya Hall. (p38)

Seattle Opera Distinguished company resident at the splendid McCaw Hall in the Seattle Center. (p71)

Music Pubs

Comet Tavern The ghosts of grunge haunt this still dive-y pub in Capitol Hill. (p87)

Owl & Thistle Fiddles, guitars and folk singers often turn up at this Irish pub in downtown. (p37)

Best
Spectator Sports

With state-of-the-art stadiums and teams that have recently won with a lot of glory, Seattle is a great town in which to watch the pros play. College games are also hugely popular with locals and a fun way to spend an afternoon.

Pro Teams

Seattle Mariners
Formed in 1977 and former tenants of the erstwhile Kingdome, the beloved baseball team plays at Safeco Field. It has yet to win a World Series title.

Seattle Seahawks The Northwest's only National Football League (NFL) franchise, the Seahawks play in 72,000-seat CenturyLink Field. The team has contested the Super Bowl twice in recent years, winning Super Bowl XLVIII in February 2014.

Seattle Sounders
Reincarnated in 2008, the soccer team has fanatical supporters and lots of 'em: 67,000 once attended a friendly against Manchester United. Highly successful, the team shares digs at CenturyLink Field with the Seahawks. The soccer season runs May to mid-September.

Sports Stadiums

CenturyLink Field Huge stadium that's home to two huge teams, football's Seahawks and soccer's Sounders. (p51)

Safeco Field The biggest temple to baseball in the Pacific Northwest; ask any Mariners fan. (p51)

☑ **Top Tips**

▶ You can buy tickets either in person at the box offices (at CenturyLink Field for soccer and American football, at Safeco Field for baseball) or online through **TicketMaster** (www. ticketmaster.com).

▶ Beware: Seattle's pro sports teams enjoy fanatical support and games regularly sell out. It is wise to book weeks, if not months, ahead.

Best
Bicycling

Seattle has become a lot more bike-friendly in recent years and took a big leap forward in 2014 when it unveiled a citywide bike-sharing scheme called Pronto. The move has been backed up with the creation of a new network of proper, dedicated bike lanes.

STEVE ESTVANIK/SHUTTERSTOCK ©

Burke-Gilman Trail

Cutting a leafy, vehicle-free path through multiple north Seattle neighborhoods, including the U District, Fremont and Ballard, the Burke-Gilman Trail is Seattle's best uninterrupted cycling path. It gets busy on sunny weekends, when cyclists overtake joggers, and skaters weave in and out of walkers and strollers. The asphalt trail was first laid out in 1978 along the path of a former railroad pioneered by two Seattle attorneys, Thomas Burke and Daniel Gilman, in 1885 (the railway ceased operation in 1971). Initially extending for 12 miles, the route has since been lengthened and now runs almost 20 miles from Kenmore on the northeast shore of Lake Washington to Golden Gardens Park in northwest Ballard.

Bike-friendly Neighborhoods

Burke-Gilman Trail
Seattle's best and most popular traffic-free cycling artery.

Alki Beach Park
Cycle the seafront from the water-taxi dock to the lighthouse. (p117)

South Lake Union
This new neighborhood has been laid out with the needs of modern cyclists in mind.

Myrtle Edwards Park
Thin strip of greenery abutting Elliott Bay that's easily accessible from downtown. (p69)

Cheshiahud Loop
Collection of paths and sidewalks that circumnavigate Lake Union. (p80)

☑ **Top Tip**

▶ Pronto, Seattle's bike-sharing scheme inaugurated in 2014, was the first of its type in the Pacific Northwest. Many locals buy annual subscriptions and borrow the bikes for their daily commute, but the scheme also offers $8 day passes, making it ideal for casual users to cycle between Seattle's more far-flung sights.

Best
Gay & Lesbian

OSCAR C WILLIAMS/SHUTTERSTOCK ©

Seattle is a progressive, liberally minded city with thriving gay and lesbian communities; census data shows that approximately 12.9% of the city's population identifies itself as gay or lesbian, and there doesn't tend to be much sexual-orientation-based hostility among the rest of the population.

Festivals & Events

TWIST: Seattle Queer Film Festival (www. threedollarbillcinema.org; ⊙Oct) is usually held in the third week of October. **Seattle Pride** (☎206-322-9561; www. seattlepride.org; ⊙Jun) is Seattle's pioneering lesbian- and gay-pride event held every year since 1974. It usually falls on the last Sunday in June and includes a huge downtown parade followed by PrideFest, during which numerous vendors and entertainers set up in the Seattle Center.

Neighbours (www.neigh boursnightclub.com; 1509 Broadway E; ⊙9am-2am

Mon, Tue & Sat, 9am-4am Thu & Fri, 10am-midnight Sun; 🚊Broadway & Pine) An always-packed dance factory for the gay club scene and its attendant glittery straight girls.

Wildrose (☎206-324-9210; 1021 E Pike St; ⊙5pm-midnight Mon, 3pm-1am Tue-Thu, 3pm-2am Fri & Sat, 3pm-midnight Sun; 🚊Broadway & Pine) Small, comfortable lesbian bar has theme nights (dykes on bikes, drag-king shows) as well as a light menu, pool, karaoke and DJs. On weekends it gets packed, so figure on a bit of a wait to get in.

Outwest Bar (☎20 6-937-1540; 5401 California Ave SW; ⊙4pm-midnight

Mon-Thu, 4pm-2am Fri & Sat, 4-10pm Sun; 🚌Rapid Ride C-Line) Proof that you don't need to gravitate to Capitol Hill to enjoy a good gay-friendly neighborhood bar, this laid-back West Seattle bar has cocktails, burgers, DJs and regular karaoke. It's about a mile south of the 'Junction' on California Ave SW.

Re-Bar (☎206-233-9873; www.rebarseattle.com; 1114 Howell St; 🚌70) Storied indie dance club in Belltown welcomes gay, straight, bi or undecided revelers to its lively dance floor. Also come for its offbeat theater, burlesque shows and poetry slams – among other wacky offerings.

Best
Activities

Never mind the rain – that's why waterproofs were invented. When you live this close to the mountains, not to mention all that water and an impressive mélange of parks, it's just criminal not to get outdoors, come rain, hail or shine. Seattle is rare for a large city in that many forms of outdoor recreation are available within the city itself.

BILL HINTON PHOTOGRAPHY/GETTY IMAGES ©

On the Water

Seeing Seattle from the water is a surefire way to fall in love with the city. A number of places rent kayaks and canoes, or you can arrange a guided tour. Sailing lessons are also available from the **Center for Wooden Boats** (p80) on Lake Union; the center also offers free 45-minute sailboat rides every Sunday morning (first come, first served).

The calmest, safest places to launch boats are Green Lake, Lake Union or near the water-taxi dock in Seacrest Park in West Seattle. If you're not confident, take a lesson. Several of the rental companies in Green Lake, Westlake (Lake Union) and the U District offer instruction from around $60 per hour.

Swimming

When summer temperatures rise, there's no more popular place to be than on one of Seattle's beaches. One of the most visited is Alki Beach in West Seattle, a real scene with beach volleyball, acres of flesh and teenagers cruising in their cars. Beware: the seawater is cold! For freshwater, Green Lake Park has two swimming and sunbathing beaches, as do several parks along the western shores of Lake Washington, including Madison, Madrona, Seward, Magnuson and Mt Baker Parks. Lifeguards are on duty at public beaches between 11am and 8pm mid-June to Labor Day (beginning of September).

☑ Top Tip

▶ **Seattle Parks & Recreation** (📞206-684-4075; www.cityofseattle.net/parks) operates four public golf courses in Seattle (green fees from around $35), along with a nine-hole pitch-and-putt course located at Green Lake, a fun spot to go if you're just learning, or lack the patience or experience to go a full round.

Washington Park Arboretum

Places to Kayak

Lake Union Dodge boats, sea-planes and ducks in Seattle's watery 'car park.' (p80)

Alki Beach Park Cast off from the beach and ponder distant Puget Sound islands. (p117)

Green Lake Park Calm, placid lake in suburban neighborhood equipped with handy boat rental concession. (p97)

Places to Jog

Discovery Park 12 miles of trails and multiple ecosystems in which to lose yourself. (p102)

Myrtle Edwards Park Join the lunchtime

hordes along the shores of Elliott Bay. (p69)

Green Lake Park Exercise central with lots of potential to overtake – or be overtaken! (p97)

Pinball

Seattle Pinball Museum One of Seattle's weirdest but most welcome museums lets you play on all the exhibits. (p46)

Flip Flip Ding Ding New bar–games room that holds regular pinball competitions. (p120)

Shorty's Belltown dive bar where pinball never went out of fashion. (p70)

Worth a Trip

The wild and lovely **Washington Park Arboretum** (🚍11), stretching from Madison Valley up to Union Bay, offers a wide variety of gardens, a wetlands nature trail and 200 acres of mature forest threaded by paths. With more than 5500 plant species growing within the arboretum's boundaries, it's a great place to walk, jog or throw a frisbee.

Best
Shopping

Seattle, like any big US city, has a whole range of big-name stores. You won't have to look for them – they'll find you. More interesting, unique and precious are the quirky, one-of-a-kind shops hidden away in some half-forgotten back alley. The city's tour de force is its bookstores and record stores, surely some of the best in the nation.

MAX HERMAN/SHUTTERSTOCK ©

Downtown Shopping

The main shopping area in Seattle is downtown between 3rd and 6th Aves and between University and Stewart Sts. You can't miss it.

For the compulsive browser, amateur chef, hungry traveler on a budget, or anyone else with their five senses fully intact, Seattle has no greater attraction than Pike Place Market. This is shopping central in Seattle: dozens of market food stalls hawk everything from geoduck clams to fennel root to harissa. Locals shop here just as much as tourists.

For the full gamut of souvenirs, simply stroll up and down the boardwalk along the waterfront.

Pot Shops

In November 2012 Washington State approved Initiative 502 by popular ballot, permitting limited marijuana use for people over the age of 21. Adults aged 21 and over may now buy up to 1oz of pure weed (or 16oz of solid edibles, or 72oz of liquid product) for private consumption in Seattle from a licensed seller. Most of the so-called 'recreational' pot shops are in the outlying districts of SoDo, Fremont and Ballard, but none of them allow customers to imbibe their products in-house.

For more information, pick up the *Green Guide*, a free magazine available in most pot shops, or peruse the special 'Weed' section of the *Stranger* newspaper.

☑ Top Tips

▶ A 9.6% sales tax is added to all purchases except food to be prepared for consumption (ie groceries).

▶ Unlike the European VAT or Canadian GST, the sales tax is not refundable to tourists.

Markets

Pike Place Market Lose yourself for a day, at least! (p26)

U District Farmers Market Produce-only market that's been running since 1993. (p110)

Ballard Farmers Market With food and some crafts, this is the place to go on a Sunday. (p110)

Pike Place Market (p26)

Shopping Strips

Pike Place Market Support your local farmer, craftsperson or third-generation store owner in Seattle's bustling heart. (p26)

Downtown Big-name stores deliver the goods in the city's retail core.

'The Ave' A dearth of designer labels but an abundance of welcome bargains beckon in the U District.

Esoterica

Market Magic Everything the young aspiring magician could dream of. (p39)

Tenzing Momo Atmospheric apothecary where

you expect to see Professor Snape jump out from behind the counter. (p39)

Card Kingdom Interactive games emporium in Ballard that could delay you for hours. (p111)

Bookstores

Metsker Maps The best travel books lurk here, including – hopefully – this one. (p38)

Globe Bookstore Tomes are piled everywhere in this old-fashioned Pioneer Square browsing room. (p52)

Fantagraphics Bookstore & Gallery Unique graphic-book store that shares digs with George-

town's best vinyl shop. (p121)

Queen Anne Book Company Small but wonderfully curated neighborhood store loved by the erudite inhabitants of Queen Anne. (p85)

Outdoor Gear

REI The flagship store of the now famous outdoor chain has a climbing wall and bike test track. (p85)

Filson Brand new outlet for classic old Seattle outfitter founded during the Klondike Gold Rush. (p52)

Best
For Kids

Take it easy, overworked parent. Seattle will entertain, pacify and often educate your energetic kid(s) without them even realizing it. Some of the attractions are obvious – a children's theater and a zoo. Others are more serendipitous: don't miss the pinball museum or the exciting urban theater of Pike Place Market.

CHERYL HANEY/EYEM/GETTY IMAGES ©

Where to Eat

Most restaurants in Seattle are kid-friendly. The only places where you're likely to see 'No Minors' signs are in pubs, gastropubs and dive bars (notwithstanding, many pubs will serve families as long as you don't sit at the bar). Some places introduce a no-kids policy after 10pm. Pike Place Market has the widest selection of cheap, immediately available food and is a fun place to hang out and eat.

Beaches

The main part of West Seattle's Alki Beach Park is sandy – ideal for sandcastle building and all of those other timeworn seaside pleasures. There are good tide pools further west around the lighthouse. Another wide sandy strip is Golden Gardens Park in the northern part of Ballard, which is home to forest trails, a children's play area and an ice cream concession.

There are other less sandy water-abutting parks on the shores of Lake Washington. Madison Park (p89) has a kids play area, plus a roped swimming area and lifeguards in the summer. The same goes for Madrona Park (p89) a mile or two further south.

Wild, wondrous Discovery Park has two long beaches, perfect for spotting wildlife and building teepees out of driftwood.

☑ Top Tips

▶ There are sometimes organized nature walks in Discovery Park. You can check schedules at the Environmental Learning Center located near the entrance.

▶ Within Discovery Park's giant green expanses you'll also find a kids play area, safe beaches and several miles of safe trails.

Eating

Beecher's Handmade Cheese Kids fall instantly in love with the mac 'n' cheese cartons. (p124)

Piroshky Piroshky Watch the flaky pastries rolled before your eyes in Pike Place Market. (p33)

Gum Wall (p28)

Top Pot Hand-Forged Doughnuts Every youthful visitor to Seattle should be allowed at least one 'treat' here. (p66)

Ivar's Acres of Clams An excellent post-aquarium fish 'n' chips lunch. (p35)

Shopping

Market Magic Pike Place Market's resident joke and magic shop. (p39)

Card Kingdom Ballard games emporium with on-site board games to buy or just play. (p111)

Animal Viewing

Woodland Park Zoo Considered one of the best zoos in the US, with 300 species including lions and tigers. (p97)

Seattle Aquarium Designed with kids in mind, the aquarium has a fish 'touching tank' and daily feeding shows. (p32)

Beach-combing

Alki Beach Park Smooth sand melding into rock pools around the headlands. (p117)

Discovery Park Wild beaches backed by cliffs and forest and littered with driftwood. (p102)

Golden Gardens Park Beach, playgrounds and grassy stretches inviting ball games. (p108)

Photo Ops

Fremont Public Sculpture A rocket sticking out of a shoe shop and a giant troll under a bridge. (p126)

Gum Wall Colorful montage to which you can add your own personal touch. (p28)

Museums

Seattle Pinball Museum Confiscate the gadgets and go retro with good old-fashioned pinball. (p46)

MoPOP Play drums and guitar in the Sound Lab or hit the Icons of Science Fiction exhibit. (p60)

Klondike Gold Rush National Historical Park Uses great storytelling to relate a swashbuckling historical episode. (p46)

Museum of Flight Experience a flight simulator and walk through Air Force One. (p114)

Best
For Free

KARL WEATHERLY/GETTY IMAGES ©

Seattle has a viable range of options to help stave off credit-card apocalypse, from the obvious (parks and public art) to the more unexpected (a market that often resembles a giant outdoor theater). To reap the best deals, head out on the first Thursday of the month when many city museums waive their entrance frees.

Fremont Public Sculpture Checking out Fremont's inspired public art costs zero and you never know what you're going to get. (p126)

Discovery Park Take bracing walks on wind-swept coastal bluffs without breaking a dollar. (p102)

Pioneer Square Historical District Study beautiful red-bricked architecture on a self-guided walking tour. (p42)

Olympic Sculpture Park Outdoor branch of Seattle Art Museum on a knoll overlooking Elliott Bay. (p66)

Klondike Gold Rush National Historical Park One of the best museums in Seat-tle – and it's free too! (p46)

Pike Place Market The market's street theater (think fish-throwers and talented buskers) will cost you nothing. (p26)

Center for Wooden Boats Free sailboat rides on Lake Union, Sunday morning at 10am; first come, first served. (p138)

Occidental Park Re-cently renovated square offering bags of free games, including ping pong, chess and table football. (p46)

Assembly Hall Belltown food emporium with a mezzanine floor offering pool and shuffleboard for *nada*. (p63)

Best
Tours

Bill Speidel's Underground Tour (☏206-682-4646; www.undergroundtour.com; 608 1st Ave; adult/senior/child $19/16/9; ⏱departs every 30min 10am-6pm Oct-Mar, 9am-7pm Apr-Sep; ☒Pioneer Sq) Tours of Seattle's historic 'Underground' buried since the 1890s start at Doc Maynard's Public House in Pioneer Square and progress through a series of subterranean walkways whose shabbiness adds to their authenticity. It is very popular and no reservations are accepted, so try to arrive 30 minutes early if you want to get in.

Seattle by Foot (☏206-508-7017; www.seattlebyfoot.com; tours $25-35) This company runs a handful of tours including the practically essential Coffee Crawl, which will ply you liberally with caffeine while explaining the nuances of latte art and dishing the inside story on the rise (and rise) of Starbucks. It costs $30 including samples. The same company also offers a unique Seattle Kids Tour; reserve ahead.

Savor Seattle (☏206-209-5485; www.savorseattletours.com) These guys lead gastronomic tours, the standout being the two-hour Booze-n-Bites that runs daily at 4pm from the corner of Western Ave and Virginia St. It costs $65 and visits culinary bastions as Von's 1000 Spirits. Prepare yourself for sublime cocktails, wine and food.

Road Dogs Seattle Brewery Tour (☏206-249-9858; www.seattlebrewerytour.com; 1425 5th Ave N; $79; ⏱tours 10:30am, 2:30pm & 6pm) Road Dogs' popular three-hour Seattle Brewery tour takes in three breweries from a list of 25, from established microbreweries to nascent nano-businesses. To allow you to safely sup samples en route, you'll be picked up and whisked around in a minibus driven by a beer expert/driver. The company also runs local coffee and distillery tours. Book online.

Fremont Tour (www.thefremonttour.com; adult/child $20/free; ⏱Jun-Sep; ☒62)

MCCATFISH/GETTY IMAGES ©

☑ **Top Tip**

▶ Free walking tours leave daily at 11am from the corner of Western Ave and Virginia St in Pike Place Market. The two-hour walk takes in Pike Pl, the waterfront and Pioneer Sq. If you have a great time (highly likely), there's a suggested $15 donation. Reserve online at www.seattlefreewalkingtours.org.

To help outsiders infiltrate Fremont's wacky underbelly, a group of enterprising locals have instituted the Fremont Tour, a 90-minute neighborhood stroll accompanied by outlandishly costumed guides. Tours meet on the corner of N 34th St and Fremont Ave N.

Best
Rainy Day Ideas

Seattle's reputation as a rainy city is well-known, if a little overblown (New York gets more rainfall). Nonetheless, with over 150 wet days a year, it's wise to come armed with plenty of rain-avoiding ideas – and an umbrella.

BRENDAN SAINSBURY/LONELY PLANET ©

Seattle Pinball Museum The best rainy day activity ever invented? (p46)

Assembly Hall Snuggle down in this tasteful indoor food emporium with coffee, light bites and copious games. (p63)

Seattle Art Museum While the downtown shoppers are getting a soaking, you can check out the Pollacks and Tobeys and keep dry. (p24)

MoPOP You won't notice (or see) the weather when you're jamming like Hendrix in the Sound Lab. (p60)

Museum of Flight Another multifarious museum that can fill half a day – or more if you're a real flying geek. (p114)

Seattle Central Library Yes, there are tons of books, but the library is also an architectural stunner. (p32)

Safeco Field Enjoy a game of pro-baseball under the shelter of the stadium's large retractable roof. (p51)

Museum of History & Industry Keep dry in the confines of a former naval armory building while learning about Seattle's past. (p74)

☑ **Top Tip**

▶ If you really can't stand the rain, come to Seattle in the months of July, August or September, which between them score an average 18 rainy days in any given year.

Survival Guide

Survival Guide

Before You Go

When to Go

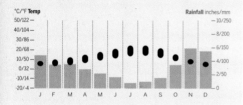

→ **Winter (Dec-Feb)**
Dreary, though rarely
super-cold, with plenty of
rainy days.

→ **Spring (Mar-May)**
Brings a few gorgeous
days. More crowded
around Easter and
during numerous May
festivals.

→ **Summer (Jun-Aug)**
Dry and sunny and thus
the best time to visit,
although you'd be wise to
book ahead.

→ **Fall (Sep-Nov)** Early
fall is less crowded than
summer but with more
changeable weather.

Book Your Stay

☑ **Top Tip** Seattle hotel
rooms are subject to a
room tax of 15.6% (less
for most B&Bs and his-
torical properties), which
will be tacked onto the
final bill.

Hotel prices in Seattle vary
considerably. For the best
deals, search around on-
line. Room prices can vary
wildly depending on:

→ Season – you can get
up to 50% off the rack
rates from November to
March; peak season is
generally May through
August.

→ Day of the week – week-
ends are usually cheaper.

→ Time of booking – ear-
lier is usually better.

→ Hotel capacity – the
fuller the hotel, the more
expensive it is.

→ Luck – are they throwing
a deal?

Useful Websites

→ **Lonely Planet** (www.
lonelyplanet.com/seattle)

destination information and reviews of Lonely Planet's top choices and bookings.

Visit Seattle (www.visitseattle.org) Deals available through the 'Lodging' page of the official Seattle/King County website.

Seattle Bed & Breakfast Association (www.lodginginseattle.com) Portal of the city's 10 best B&Bs.

Best Budget

Moore Hotel (www.moorehotel.com) Cheap, historic and perfectly comfortable bargain option on the cusp of downtown.

Hotel Hotel Hostel (www.hotelhotel.co) Fremont's only non-B&B accommodation – a kind of hipster hostel with industrial-chic decor.

City Hostel Seattle (www.hostelseattle.com) Hostel with private options and good wall art in Belltown.

Green Tortoise Hostel (www.greentortoise.net) Seattle's favorite backpacker haunt location across the street from Pike Place Market.

Best Midrange

Edgewater (www.edgewaterhotel.com) A hotel steeped in rock history that juts out over Elliott Bay.

Hotel Max (www.hotelmaxseattle.com) Boutique hotel with an art and music theme on the cusp of Belltown and downtown.

University Inn (www.universityinnseattle.com) Close to the university, but a long way from austere student digs.

Palladian Hotel (www.palladianhotel.com) Big boutique hotel in Belltown with funky rock-star wall art.

Best Top End

Hotel Monaco (www.monaco-seattle.com) Lavish downtown hotel with refreshingly down-to-earth service.

Fairmont Olympic Hotel (www.fairmont.com/seattle) Seattle's jazz-age giant rolls out the red carpet in downtown.

Arctic Club (www.thearcticclubseattle.com) Commodious throwback to the age of the gold rush.

Arriving in Seattle

Sea-Tac International Airport

Sound Transit (www.soundtransit.org) runs the Central Link light rail service between the city center and the airport. Trains go every 15 minutes or better between 5am and just after midnight. The ride between the Westlake Center (downtown) and Sea-Tac takes 37 minutes and costs $3.

Shuttle Express (📞 425-981-7000; www.shuttleexpress.com) has a pickup and drop-off point on the 3rd floor of the airport garage; it charges approximately $18 and is handy if you have a lot of luggage.

Taxis are available at the parking garage on the 3rd floor. Fares to downtown start at $42.

Rental-car counters are located in the baggage-claim area.

Driving into Seattle from the airport is fairly

straightforward – just take I-5 north.

King Street Station

➤ **First Hill streetcar** runs from near King Street Station through the International District and First Hill to Capitol Hill every 15 minutes. Fares are $2.25/1.50 per adult/child.

➤ **Central Link's light rail station** International District/Chinatown is adjacent to King Street station. From here it is three stops (seven minutes) to the Westlake Center in downtown. Fares are $2.25/1.50 per adult/child.

The Piers

➤ **Metro buses** 24 and 19 connect Pier 91 in Magnolia with downtown via the Seattle Center. Fares are a flat $2.75.

➤ **Shuttle Express** (☏425-981-7000; www. shuttleexpress.com) links the piers with Sea-Tac airport ($22) or downtown ($7).

➤ **Driving** to Pier 52 for the car ferries, leave I-5 at exit 164A (northbound) or exit 165B (southbound).

Getting Around

....

Light Rail

☑ **Best for...**Getting from downtown to outlying areas like the airport and the U District.

➤ **Sound Transit** (www. soundtransit.org) operates Link light rail. The first – and, as yet, only – Seattle line, Central Link, runs from Sea-Tac airport to the University of Washington via Westlake Station in downtown.

➤ **Fares** within the city limits are $2.25. From downtown to the airport costs $3. Trains run between 5am and 12:30am.

Streetcar

☑ **Best for...**Sightseeing, fun and getting around South Lake Union and First Hill.

➤ **Seattle Streetcar** (www. seattlestreetcar.org) has two lines: the 2.6-mile South Lake Union line that runs between the Westlake Center and Lake Union; and the First Hill line, which opened in 2016 and runs from Pioneer Square via the International

District and First Hill to Capitol Hill.

➤ **Fares** cost a standard $2.25/1.50 per adult/child. Streetcars breeze by every 15 minutes from 6am to 9pm (slightly later on Friday and Saturday).

Bus

☑ **Best for...**Short hops and getting to some of Seattle's outlying sights and neighborhoods.

➤ **King County Metro Transit** (☏206-553-3000; www.metro.kingcounty.gov) operates Seattle's buses. The website prints schedules and maps and has a trip planner.

➤ **Fares** within Seattle city limits are a flat $2.75 at peak hours (6am to 9am and 3pm to 6pm weekdays); off-peak rates are $2.50. Those aged six to 18 pay $1.50, kids under six years are free, and seniors and travelers with disabilities pay $1.

➤ **Rapid Ride buses** (labeled A to F) are faster and more frequent (every 10 minutes). Of interest to travelers are lines C (downtown to West Seattle) and D (downtown to Ballard).

icycle

Best for... Exercise, hort hops and navigating raffic-calmed neighborhoods like South Lake nion.

Pronto Cycle Share 🎜844-677-6686; www. ontocycleshare.com) is eattle's bike-sharing cheme. It covers most f the central area of ne city. There are 500 vailable bikes located 54 docking stations. 24-hour Pronto pass osts $8 and is payable t machines at any station. You also have the ption to rent mandatory helmets.

Bike lanes all around ne city have improved xponentially since the ntroduction of Pronto ack in 2014. They re painted green and sually separated from raffic lanes.

rivate Vehicle

🎜 **Best for...** Arriving nly! Get around town y public transportation r bike.

eattle traffic is disroportionately heavy nd chaotic for a city f its size, and parking s generally scarce and xpensive. Add to that ne city's bizarrely

cobbled-together mishmash of skewed grids, the hilly terrain and the preponderance of oneway streets and it's easy to see why driving downtown is best avoided if at all possible.

Essential Information

Business Hours

Banks 9am or 10am to 5pm or 6pm weekdays; some also 10am to 2pm Saturday

Businesses 9am to 5pm or 6pm weekdays; some also 10am to 5pm Saturday

Restaurants Breakfast 7am to 11am, brunch 7am to 3pm, lunch 11:30am to 2:30pm, dinner 5:30pm to 10pm

Shops 9am or 10am to 5pm or 6pm (or 9pm in shopping malls) weekdays, noon to 5pm (later in malls) weekends; some places open till 8pm or 9pm

Electricty

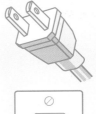

120V/60Hz

120V/60Hz

Emergency

The Community Information Line (🎜20 6-461-3200) provides

information on emergency services, housing, legal advice etc.

Country Code	☎1
Police, Fire & Ambulance	☎911
Seattle Police	☎206-625-5011
Washington State Patrol	☎360-596-2600

Money

☑ **Top Tip** Tipping is a way of life in the US and not optional.

➡ The US dollar is divided into 100 cents. US coins come in denominations of 1c (penny), 5c (nickel), 10c (dime), 25c (quarter), the practically extinct 50c (half-dollar) and the not-often-seen golden dollar coin.

➡ Notes come in $1, $5, $10, $20, $50 and $100 denominations.

ATMs

ATMs are easy to find: there's practically one per block in the busier commercial areas, as well as one outside every bank.

Changing Money

➡ Banks and money-changers will give you US currency based on the current exchange rate.

➡ **Travelex-Thomas Cook Currency Services** (⊙6am-8pm) The booth at the main airport terminal is behind the Delta Airlines counter.

Credit & Debit Cards

Major credit cards are accepted at most hotels, restaurants and shops throughout Seattle. Places that accept Visa and MasterCard generally also accept (and will often prefer) debit cards, which deduct payments directly from your check or savings account.

Public Holidays

National public holidays are celebrated throughout the USA. On public holidays banks, schools and government offices (including post offices) are closed and public transportation follows a Sunday schedule.

New Year's Day January 1

Martin Luther King Jr Day Third Monday in January

Presidents' Day Third Monday in February

Memorial Day Last Monday in May

Independence Day (Fourth of July) July 4

Labor Day First Monday in September

Columbus Day Second Monday in October

Veterans' Day November 11

Thanksgiving Day Fourth Thursday in November

Christmas Day December 25

Telephone

➡ Phone numbers within the USA consist of a three-digit area code followed by a seven-digit local number.

➡ If you're calling long distance, dial ☎1 plus the three-digit area code plus the seven-digit number.

➡ To call internationally, first dial ☎011 then the country code and phone number.

➡ Phone numbers in Seattle have a ☎206 area code. Even local calls made to the same area code require you to dial the full 10-digit number (no need to dial ☎1 first, though).

Tourist Information

☑ **Top Tip** Most hotels stock a useful stash of tourist brochures.

sit Seattle (🖉 20
461-5800; www.visitseattle.
g; cnr Pike St & 7th Ave,
ashington State Convention
enter; ⏰9am-5pm daily
n-Sep, Mon-Fri Oct-May;
Westlake) The main
urist information center
located in the Wash-
gton State Convention
enter in downtown.

ravelers with isabilities

All public buildings
ncluding all hotels,
staurants, theaters and
useums) are required
law to provide wheel-
air access and to have
propriate restroom
cilities available.

Telephone companies
ovide relay operators
the hearing impaired.

Many banks provide
M instructions in braille.

Around 80% of Metro's
ses are equipped
th wheelchair lifts.

Timetables marked with
an 'L' indicate wheelchair
accessibility.

➡ Most large private
and chain hotels have
suites for guests with
disabilities.

➡ Many car-rental agen-
cies offer hand-controlled
models at no extra
charge.

➡ All major airlines, Grey-
hound buses and Amtrak
trains allow guide dogs to
accompany passengers
and often sell two-for-one
packages when attend-
ants of passengers with
serious disabilities are
required.

Visas

☑ For updates on visas
and other security issues,
you can visit the US De-
partment of State website
(www.travel.state.gov).

➡ Foreigners needing
visas to travel to the US
should plan ahead. There
is a reciprocal visa-waiver

program (better known
as ESTA) in which citizens
of 38 countries may
enter the USA for stays
of 90 days or less with
a passport but without
first obtaining a visa.
Currently these countries
include Australia, Japan,
Switzerland the UK, and
the EU. Under this pro-
gram you can stay in the
USA for up to 90 days.

➡ Citizens of countries
in the US Visa Waiver
Program have to register
with the government on-
line (https://esta.cbp.dhs.
gov) three days before
their visit. The registra-
tion is valid for two years
and costs $14.

➡ Canadian citizens do
not need a visa or a visa
waiver to travel to the US.

➡ Other travelers will
need to obtain a visa from
a US consulate or em-
bassy. In most countries,
the process can be done
by mail.

Behind the Scenes

Send Us Your Feedback

We love to hear from travelers – your comments help make our books better. We read every word, and we guarantee that your feedback goes straight to the authors. Visit **lonelyplanet.com/contact** to submit your updates and suggestions.

Note: We may edit, reproduce and incorporate your comments in Lonely Planet products such as guidebooks, websites and digital products, so let us know if you don't want your comments reproduced or your name acknowledged. For a copy of our privacy policy visit lonelyplanet.com/privacy.

Brendan's Thanks

Thanks to all the untold bus drivers, chefs, hotel receptionists, tour guides and innocent bystanders who helped me during this research. Special thanks to my wife, Liz, and ten-year-old son, Kieran, for their company on the road.

Acknowledgements

Cover photograph: MoPOP, Seattle Center; Urban Texture/Alamy©

This Book

This 1st edition of Lonely Planet's *Pocket Seattle* guidebook was researched and written by Brendan Sainsbury. This guidebook was produced by the following:

Destination Editor Alexander Howard

Product Editors Sandie Kestell, Kate Mathews

Senior Cartographer Alison Lyall

Book Designer Gwen Cotter

Assisting Editors Michelle Bennett, Lauren O'Connell

Cover Researcher Naomi Parker

Thanks to Carolyn Bain, Jennifer Carey, Evan Godt, Genna Patterson, Jessica Ryan, Angela Tinson, Tony Wheeler, Dora Whitaker

Index

See also separate subindexes for:

🚫 **Eating p157**

🍺 **Drinking p158**

✪ **Entertainment p158**

🔒 **Shopping p159**

Sights 000
Map Pages **000**

😕 Eating

Our Writer

Brendan Sainsbury

Born and raised in the UK in a town that never merits a mention in any guidebook (Andover, Hampshire), Brendan spent the holidays of his youth caravanning in the English Lake District and didn't leave Blighty until he was 19. Making up for lost time, he's since squeezed 70 countries into a sometimes precarious existence as a writer and professional vagabond. His rocking chair memories will probably include staging a performance of 'A Comedy of Errors' at a school in war-torn Angola, running 150 miles across the Sahara Desert in the Marathon des Sables, and hitchhiking from Cape Town to Kilimanjaro with an early, dog-eared copy of LP's *Africa on a Shoestring*. In the last 11 years, he has written over 40 books for Lonely Planet from Castro's Cuba to the canyons of Peru. When not scribbling research notes, Brendan likes partaking in ridiculous 'endurance' races, strumming old Clash songs on the guitar, and experiencing the pain and occasional pleasures of following Southampton Football Club.

Published by Lonely Planet Global Limited
CRN 554153
1st edition – June 2017
ISBN 978 1 78657 702 3
© Lonely Planet 2017   Photographs © as indicated 2017
10 9 8 7 6 5 4 3 2 1
Printed in China

Although the authors and Lonely Planet have taken all reasonable care in preparing this book, we make no warranty about the accuracy or completeness of its content and, to the maximum extent permitted, disclaim all liability arising from its use.